Introducing Blockchain with Java

Program, Implement, and Extend Blockchains with Java

Spiro Buzharovski

Apress®

Introducing Blockchain with Java: Program, Implement, and Extend Blockchains with Java

Spiro Buzharovski
Skopje, North Macedonia

ISBN-13 (pbk): 978-1-4842-7926-7 ISBN-13 (electronic): 978-1-4842-7927-4
https://doi.org/10.1007/978-1-4842-7927-4

Managing Director, Apress Media LLC: Welmoed Spahr
Acquisitions Editor: Steve Anglin
Development Editor: Laura Berendson
Coordinating Editor: Mark Powers
Copy Editor: Kim Wimpsett

Cover designed by eStudioCalamar

Cover image by Fre Sonneveld on Unsplash (www.unsplash.com)

Distributed to the book trade worldwide by Apress Media, LLC, 1 New York Plaza, New York, NY 10004, U.S.A. Phone 1-800-SPRINGER, fax (201) 348-4505, e-mail orders-ny@springer-sbm.com, or visit www.springeronline.com. Apress Media, LLC is a California LLC and the sole member (owner) is Springer Science + Business Media Finance Inc (SSBM Finance Inc). SSBM Finance Inc is a **Delaware** corporation.

For information on translations, please e-mail booktranslations@springernature.com; for reprint, paperback, or audio rights, please e-mail bookpermissions@springernature.com.

Apress titles may be purchased in bulk for academic, corporate, or promotional use. eBook versions and licenses are also available for most titles. For more information, reference our Print and eBook Bulk Sales web page at http://www.apress.com/bulk-sales.

Any source code or other supplementary material referenced by the author in this book is available to readers on GitHub (https://github.com/Apress). For more detailed information, please visit http://www.apress.com/source-code.

Printed on acid-free paper

Dedicated to my friends.

Table of Contents

About the Author

Spiro Buzharovski is a full-stack software developer in the IT sector. He has a degree in mechanical engineering and has worked as an engineer in the oil and gas sector for more than six years. His interests include Java frameworks, blockchain, and the latest high-tech trends. Inspiration for this book came while working as a technical reviewer on an Apress book by Boro Sitnikovski, *Introducing Blockchain with Lisp: Implement and Extend Blockchains with the Racket Language.*

About the Technical Reviewer

Filip Tanurovski is a senior software engineer with more than eight years of experience. He has a degree in informatics and computer engineering. During the first five years of his career, he primarily worked as a web developer using the Java technology stack, although, lately, he has switched his focus to other technologies like Node.js, Python, and Ruby, to name a few. For two years, he was a course instructor for a five-week introductory course to Java. He became passionate about writing clean and maintainable code after reading the works of Robert Martin (Uncle Bob). He is a highly motivated individual who is constantly looking for ways to improve himself. In his spare time, he likes to spend time with his wife, family, and friends, to travel, and train kickboxing.

Preface

This book is for anyone with at least entry-level knowledge of Java or a similar OOP language, entry-level knowledge of FXML or HTML or similar markup languages, and entry-level knowledge of SQL. The book will provide a solid understanding of blockchains and a great portfolio project for those seeking employment as a developer in the blockchain space or other IT sectors. It is great for developers who want to learn by doing.

Chapter 1 is an excerpt from *Introducing Blockchain with Lisp: Implement and Extend Blockchains with the Racket Language* by Boro Sitnikovski. I am most grateful to Boro for allowing me to reuse his first chapter here. It explains the theoretical part with excellent clarity, and I feel very fortunate to have it included in my book. The rest of the book will offer a step-by-step guide of how to create your own crypto coin by implementing Blockchain technology in Java. This book contains a completely unique implementation of a blockchain in the Java language. Also, it will teach you how to create a basic user interface using JavaFX and how to implement an SQLite database using a JDBC driver for our blockchain. These topics will greatly help in visualizing the final product and provide you with a solid set of transferable technical skills.

The recommended approach for the book is to follow along with each chapter and write the code as it's being explained instead of reading passively. This way you will get the most from this book. All of the source code is available for download from `https://github.com/5pir3x/e-coin`. You should look at this book as a guide to the why and how of the codebase found in the repository.

Feel free to contact me at `spirobuzarovski@yahoo.com` for any questions you might have, and I will do my best to answer.

Finally, thank you for purchasing this book! I hope this book will dispel a lot of the mysteries surrounding the blockchain and that it will spark some more interest in Java and blockchain technology.

CHAPTER 1

Introduction to Blockchain

The entirety of this chapter is comprised of an excerpt from Introducing Blockchain with Lisp: Implement and Extend Blockchains with the Racket Language *by Boro Sitnikovski, and it is reused here with the author's permission.*

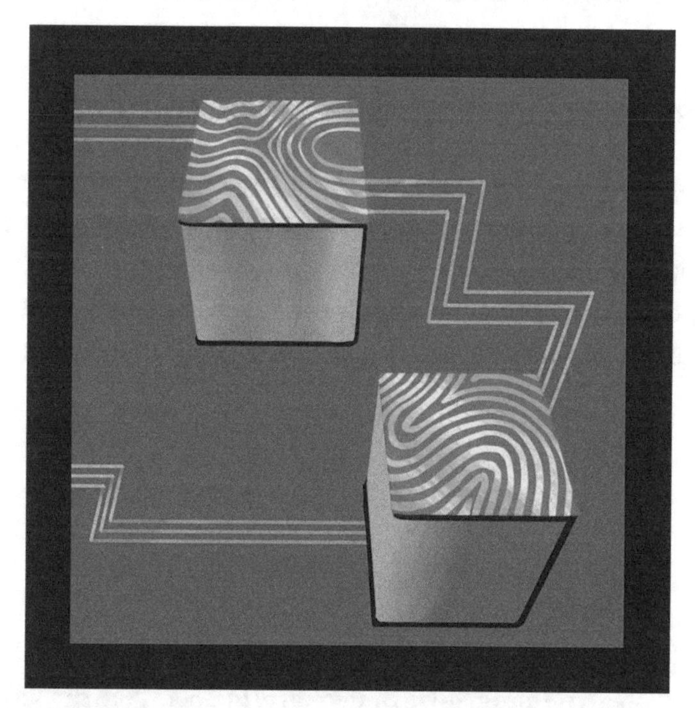

"Chained" by Filip Rizov

S. Buzharovski, *Introducing Blockchain with Java*,
https://doi.org/10.1007/978-1-4842-7927-4_1

In this chapter, we will see some definitions and examples for blockchain. We will see what properties a blockchain has, what it allows us to do, and what it is good for.

Definition 1-1 *Blockchain* is a system in which a record of transactions is maintained across several computers that are linked in a peer-to-peer network.[1]

We will give an example that will serve as motivation, as well as define what encryption and hashing techniques are and how they will help us with our system.

Note that we will skip some of the technical bits in this chapter, as it is only supposed to serve as introductory material. The technical bits will be covered later when we start building the blockchain.

1.1 Motivation and Basic Definitions

Let's assume that you and your friends exchange money often, for example, paying for dinner or drinks. It can be inconvenient to exchange cash all the time.

One possible solution is to keep records of all the bills that you and your friends have. This is called a *ledger* and is depicted in Figure 1-1.

[1] We will use this definition throughout the book, but note that there are many different definitions on the Internet. By the end of this book, you should be able to distinguish the slight nuances and similarities in each definition.

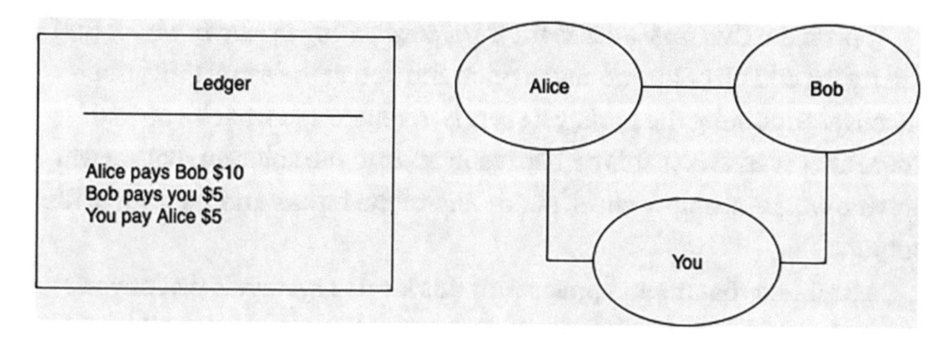

Figure 1-1. *A ledger and a set of connected friends (peers)*

Definition 1-2 A *ledger* is a book that contains a record of transactions.

Further, at the end of every day, you all sit together and refer to the ledger to do the calculations to settle up. Let's imagine that there is a pot that is the place where all of the money is kept. If you spent more than you received, you put that money in the pot; otherwise, you take that money out.

We want to design the system such that it functions similarly to a regular bank account. A holder of a wallet (bank account) should be able to only send money from their wallet to other wallets. Thus, every person in the system will have a wallet of a kind, which can also be used to determine the balance for them. Note that with the current setup using a ledger, we have to go through all the existing records to determine the balance of a specific wallet.

If we want to avoid going through all the existing records, there is a way we can optimize this with *unspent transaction outputs* (UTXOs), as we will see later in Chapter 3.

A problem that may arise is the *double-spending problem*, where Bob can try to send all of his money to Alice and you at the same time, thus effectively doubling the money he sends in relation to what he owned. There are several ways this can be resolved, and the solution that we will provide will be a simple check of the sum of the inputs and the sum of the outputs.

A problem that might appear with this kind of system is that anyone can add a transaction. For example, Bob can add a transaction where Alice pays him a few dollars without Alice's approval. We need to re-think our system such that each transaction will have a way to be verified/signed.

Definition 1-3 A *digital signature* is a way to verify the authenticity of digital messages or documents.

For signing and verifying transactions we will rely on digital signatures (Figure 1-2). For now, let's assume that anyone who adds information to the ledger also adds a signature with each record, and others have no way to modify the signature, but only to verify it. We will cover the technical details in the "Encryption" section.

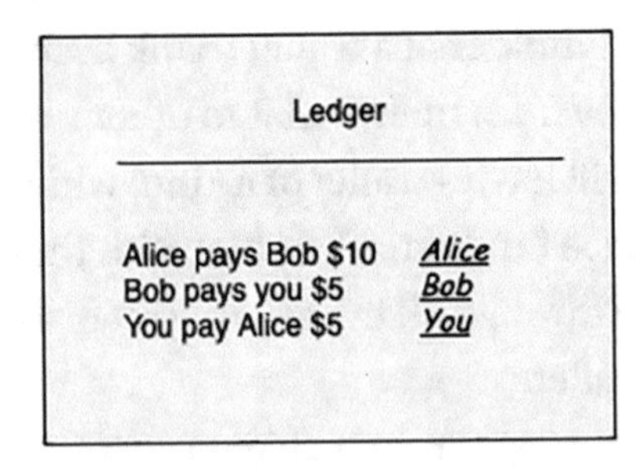

***Figure 1-2.** Our ledger now contains signatures*

However, let's assume that Bob is keeping the ledger to himself, and everybody agrees to this. The ledger is now stored in what is a centralized place. But in this case, if Bob is unavailable at the end of the day when everybody gathers to settle up, nobody will be able to refer to the ledger.

We need a way to decentralize the ledger, such that at any given time any of the people can do a transaction. For this, every person involved will keep a copy of the ledger to themselves, and when they meet at the end of the day, they will sync their ledgers.

You are connected to your friends, and so are they to you. Informally, this makes a peer-to-peer network.

Definition 1-4 A *peer-to-peer network* is formed when two or more computers are connected to each other.

For example, when you are accessing a web page on the Internet using a browser, your browser is the *client*, and the web page you're accessing is hosted by a *server*. This represents a centralized system since every user is getting the information from a single place—the *server*.

In contrast, in a peer-to-peer network, which represents a decentralized system, the distinction between a client and a server is blurred. Every peer is both a client and a server at the same time.

With the system (Figure 1-3), as the list of peers (people) grows, we might run into a problem of trust. When everybody meets at the end of the day to sync their ledgers, how can they believe the others that the transactions listed in their ledgers are true? Even if everybody trusts everybody else for their ledger, what if a new person wants to join this network? It's natural for existing users to ask this newcomer to prove that they can be trusted. We need to modify our system to support this kind of trust. One way to achieve that is through so-called *proof of work*, which we introduce next.

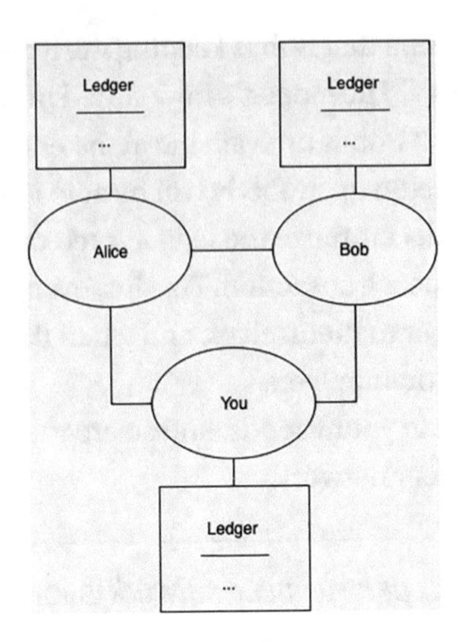

Figure 1-3. *A decentralized ledger*

Definition 1-5 A *proof of work* is data that is time-consuming to calculate and easy for others to verify.

For each record we will also include a special number (or a *hash*) that will represent proof of work, in that it will provide proof that the transaction is valid. We will cover the technical details in the "Hashing" section.

At the end of the day, we agree that we will trust the ledger of the person who has put most of the work in it. If Bob has some errands to run, he can catch up the next day by trusting the rest of the peers in the network.

In addition to all this, we want the transactions to have an order, so every record will also contain a link to the previous record. This represents the actual blockchain, depicted in Figure 1-4.

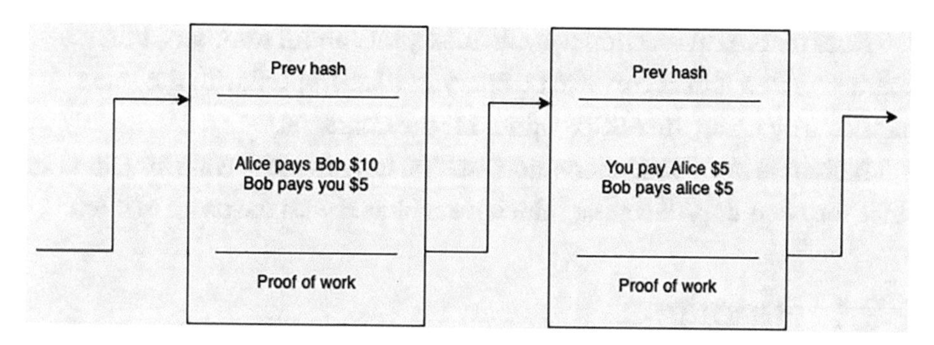

Figure 1-4. *A chain of blocks: blockchain*

If everybody agreed to use this ledger as a source of truth, there would be no need to exchange physical money at all. Everybody can just use the ledger to put in or retrieve money from it.

To understand the technical bits of digital signatures and proof of work, we will be looking at encryption and hashing, respectively. Fortunately for us, the programming language that we will be using has built-in functionalities for encryption and hashing. We don't have to dig too deep into how hashing and encryption and decryption work, but a basic understanding of them will be sufficient.

Observe how we started with a simple definition of a ledger and gradually built up to a complex system. We will use the same approach in programming.

1.2 Encryption

We will start with the following definition.

Definition 1-6 *Encryption* is a method of encoding values such that only authorized people can view the original content. Decryption is a method of decoding encrypted values.

Note that in this section we will mostly talk about numbers, but characters and letters can also be encrypted/decrypted with the same methods, by using the ASCII[2] values for the characters.

Before we talk about encryption, we first have to recall what functions are, since the encoding/decoding values are achieved with the usage of them.

1.2.1 Functions

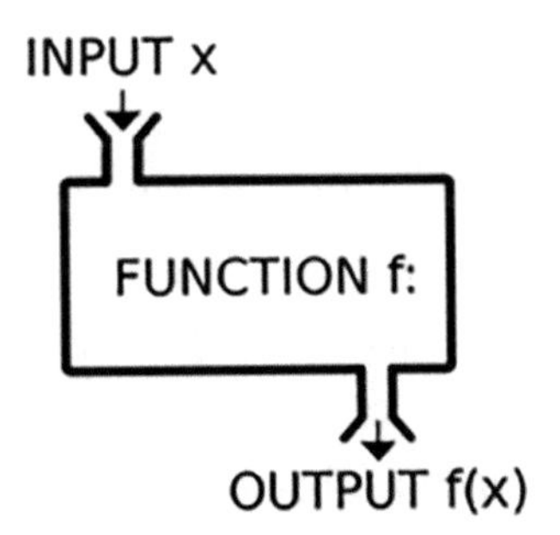

Figure 1-5. *A function*

Definition 1-7 *Functions* are mathematical entities that assign unique outputs to given inputs.

For example, you might have a function that accepts as input a person and as output returns the person's age or name. Another example is the function $f(x) = x + 1$. There are many inputs this function can accept: 1, 2, 3.14. For example, when we input 2, it gives us an output of 3, since $f(2) = 2 + 1 = 3$.

[2] An ASCII table is a table that assigns a unique number to each character (such as !, @, a, Z, etc.).

One simple way to think of functions is in the form of tables. For a function $f(x)$ accepting a single argument x, we have a two-column table where the first column is the input, and the second column is the output. For a function $f(x, y)$ accepting two arguments x and y, we have a three-column table where the first and second columns represent the input, and the third column is the output. Thus, to display the function discussed earlier in the form of a table, it would look like this:

x*f*	(*x*)
1	2
2	3
...	...

1.2.2 Symmetric-Key Algorithm

We can assume that there exist functions $E(x)$ and $D(x)$ for encryption and decryption, respectively. We want these functions to have the following properties:

- `E(x)` $\neq$ `x`, meaning that the encrypted value should not be the same as the original value
- `E(x)` $\neq$ `D(x)`, meaning that the encryption and decryption functions produce different values
- `D(E(x)) = x`, meaning that the decryption of an encrypted value should return the original value

For example, let's assume there's some kind of an encryption scheme, say `E("Boro") = 426f726f`. We can "safely" communicate the value 426f726f without actually exposing our original value, and only those who know the decryption scheme `D(x)` will be able to see that `D(426f726f) = "Boro"`.

Another example of encryption scheme is for E(x) to shift every character in x forward, and for `D(x)` to shift every character in x backward. This scheme is known as the Caesar cipher. To encrypt the text "abc" we have `E("abc") = "bcd"`, and to decrypt it we have `D("bcd") = "abc"`.

However, the scheme described makes a symmetric algorithm (Figure 1-6), meaning that we have to share the functions `E` and `D` with the parties involved, and as such, they may be open to attacks.

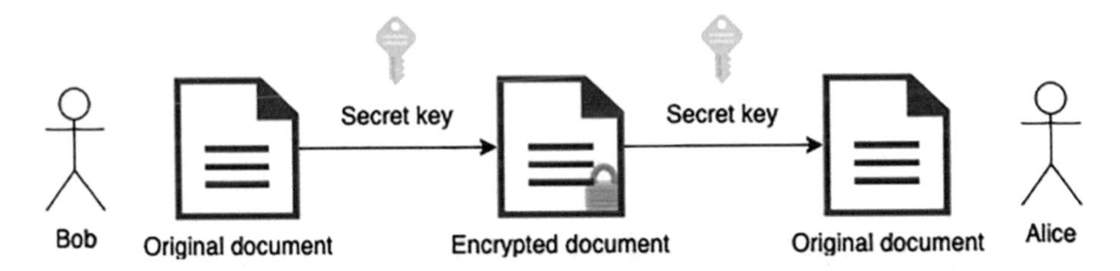

Figure 1-6. *Symmetric-key algorithm*

1.2.3 Asymmetric-Key Algorithm

To solve the problems that arise with symmetric-key algorithms, we will use what is called an *asymmetric algorithm* or *public-key cryptography* (Figure 1-7). In this scheme, we have two kinds of keys: public and private. We share the public key with the world and keep the private one to ourselves.

Figure 1-7. *Asymmetric-key algorithm*

This algorithm scheme has a neat property where only the private key can decode a message, and the public key can encode a message.

We have two functions that should have the same properties as those for the symmetric-key algorithm.

- `E(x, p)`, which encrypts a message `x` given a public key `p`
- `D(x′ , s)`, which decrypts an encrypted message `x′` given a private (secret) key `s`

In our example, we will rely on the modulo operation. Recall that $a \bmod b$ represents the remainder when a is divided by b. For example, $4 \bmod 2 = 0$ because there is no remainder when dividing 4 by 2; however, $5 \bmod 2 = 1$.

Here's one example of a basic encryption algorithm based on addition and modulo operations:

1. Pick one random number, for example 100. This will represent a common, publicly available key.
2. Pick another random number in the range (1, 100), for example 97. This will represent the private key `s`.
3. The public key `p` is obtained by subtracting the common key from the private: $100 - 97 = 3$.
4. To encrypt data, add it to the public key and take modulo 100: `E(x, p) = (x + p) mod 100`.
5. To decrypt data, we use the same logic but with our private key, so `D(x′ , s) = (x′ + s) mod 100`.

For example, suppose we want to encrypt 5. Then `E(5, 3) = (5 + 3) mod 100 = 8`. To decrypt 8, we have `D(8, 97) = (8 + 97) mod 100 = 105 mod 100 = 5`.

This example uses a very simple generation pair of `(x + y) mod c`. But, in practice, the pair generation algorithm is much more complex and harder to break by attackers. After all, the complexity of the algorithm's computation is what makes it hard to break it.

We can use a similar algorithm for digital signatures:

- `S(x, s)`, which signs a message `x` given a private key `s` (encryption)
- `V (x′ , sig, p)`, which verifies a signed message `x′`, given signature `sig` and public key `p` (decryption)

As we said earlier, each record will also include a special number (or a hash). This hash will be what is produced by `S(x, s)` (encryption). A hash can be verified by using the verify function to confirm a record's ownership (decryption).

The wallet will contain a pair of public and a private key. These keys will be used to receive or send money. With the private key, it is possible to write new blocks (or transactions) to the blockchain, effectively spending money. With the public key, others can send currency and verify signatures.

EXERCISE 1-1

Come up with a table of functions such that:

1. The input is a number, and the output is a number
2. The input is a number, and the output is the name of an employee in a company given that number

EXERCISE 1-2

Check the three properties for a symmetric-key algorithm to ensure the Caesar cipher is compatible with them.

EXERCISE 1-3

Come up with an encryption scheme, based on mathematical substitution.

EXERCISE 1-4

Use the asymmetric-key algorithm we defined to sign a message and verify it.

Hint This is similar to the encryption/decryption example shown earlier.

1.3 Hashing

Definition 1-8 Hashing is a one-way function in that it encodes text without a way to retrieve the original value.

Hashing is simpler than the previously described encryption schemes. One example of a hashing function is to return the length of characters as in `H ("abc") = 3`, but also `H ("bcd") = 3`. This means we don't have a way to retrieve the original value just by using the return value 3.

As we mentioned earlier, the reason to use such a technique is that it has some interesting properties, such as providing us with the proof of work.

Definition 1-9 *Mining* is the process of validating transactions. For this effort, successful miners obtain money as a reward.

Hashcash is one kind of a proof-of-work system.[3] We will use it to implement mining. We will see how this algorithm works in detail in the later chapters where we will implement it.

Hashing functions have another useful property that allows connecting two or more distinct blocks by having the information about the current block's hash (current hash) and previous block's hash (previous hash) in each block. For example, block-1 may have a hash such as 123456, and block-2 may have a hash such as 345678. Now, block-2's previous-hash will be block-1's current hash, that is, 123456. Here, we linked these two blocks, thus effectively creating a linked list of blocks containing ledgers with transactions. Figure 1-4 depicts this linking.

The hash of the block is based on the block's data itself, so to verify a hash we can just hash the block's data and compare it to current hash.

Two or more blocks (or transactions) that are connected form a blockchain. The validity of the blockchain will depend on the validity of each transaction.

EXERCISE 1-5

Come up with your own hashing function.

EXERCISE 1-6

In which way can the linked list depicted in Figure 1-4 be traversed? What are the implications of this property?

[3] Hashcash was initially targeted for limiting email spam and other attacks. However, recently it's also become known for its usage in blockchains as part of the mining process. Hashcash was proposed in 1997 by Adam Backa.

1.4 Smart Contracts

Definition 1-10 A *smart contract* is a self-executing contract with the conditions of an agreement between a buyer and a seller being directly written into lines of code.

A blockchain is programmable if the transactions themselves can be programmed by users. For example, users (not necessarily programmers) can write a script to add additional requirements that must be satisfied before sending money. It could look something like this:

```
1     if (user has  more  than 10  money)
2            then  approve transaction
3            else reject transaction
```

Smart contracts are implemented as a computation that takes place on the blockchain.

1.5 Bitcoin

Bitcoin was the world's first implementation of a blockchain. In November 2008, a link to a paper authored by Satoshi Nakamoto titled "Bitcoin: A Peer-to-Peer Electronic Cash System" was published on a cryptography mailing list. Bitcoin's white paper consists of nine pages; however, it is a mostly theoretical explanation of the design and as such may be a bit overwhelming to newcomers.

The Bitcoin software is open source code and was released in January 2009 on SourceForge. The design of a Bitcoin includes a decentralized network (peer-to-peer network), block (mining), blockchain, transactions, and wallets, each of which we will look at in detail in this book.

Although there are many blockchain models and each one of them differs in implementation details, the blockchain we will be building upon in this book will look pretty similar to Bitcoin, with some parts simplified.

1.6 Example Workflows

We will list a few important workflows that our system will use, among others.

Mining a block creates a new block, using Hashcash to calculate the current hash of the block. It also contains the previous hash that is a link to the previous block in the blockchain.

Checking a wallet balance for person A will first filter all blocks in the blockchain (sender = A or receiver = A) and then sum them to calculate the balance. The more our blockchain grows, the longer this operation will take. For that purpose, we will use unspent transaction outputs or the UTXO model. This model is a list of transactions containing information about the owner and the amount of money. Thus, every transaction will consume elements from this list.

Adding a block to a blockchain consists of sending money from A to B. One prerequisite is that A has enough money; we check this using the wallet balance workflow. We proceed by creating a transaction (sender = A, receiver = B) and signing it. Then we mine a block using this transaction and update the UTXO with the rewards.

1.7 Summary

The point of this chapter is to get a vague idea of how the system that we will implement looks. Things will become much clearer in the next chapter where we will be explicit about the definitions of every entity.

Here's what we learned in this chapter, briefly:

- The core entity of the system is a block.
- A block contains (among other data) transactions.
- We have a ledger that is an ordered list of all valid blocks (blockchain.)
- Every peer involved with the ledger has a wallet.
- Every record in the ledger is signed by the owner and can be verified by the public (digital signatures).
- The ledger is in a decentralized location; that is, everybody has a copy of it.
- Trust is based upon proof of work (mining).

CHAPTER 2

Model: Blockchain Core

"Block" by Filip Rizov

S. Buzharovski, *Introducing Blockchain with Java*,
https://doi.org/10.1007/978-1-4842-7927-4_2

Now that we have explained in theory what a blockchain is and how it is useful, the next obvious step is to start implementing it in Java. In this chapter, we will start by creating the model classes that represent the most elementary building blocks for our application. You can either look at the code snippets provided or download the complete repository from `https://github.com/5pir3x/e-coin`. The exercises included will offer insight and give you ideas for you to modify my code to create alternative implementations of various aspects of the application. I urge you to try to complete as many of them as possible; my hope is that at the end you will have not only a greater and deeper understanding of blockchain technology but also with a great project for your portfolio that's an alternative to my implementation instead of a mere copy. I have chosen to create a folder named `Model` inside my `src.com.company` folder structure in my repository and keep my model classes there. It is recommended that you choose the same folder structure for your project to avoid any pathing or import problems.

2.1 Block.java

We will start first by listing the imports in the following code snippet:

```
1  package com.company.Model;
2
3  import sun.security.provider.DSAPublicKeyImpl;
4
5  import java.io.Serializable;
6  import java.security.InvalidKeyException;
7  import java.security.Signature;
8  import java.security.SignatureException;
9  import java.util.ArrayList;
10 import java.util.Arrays;
11 import java.util.LinkedList;
12
```

Next we move on to our class declaration and fields, as shown in our next code snippet:

```
13 public class Block implements Serializable {
14
15      private byte[] prevHash;
16      private byte[] currHash;
17      private String timeStamp;
18      private byte[] minedBy;
19      private Integer ledgerId = 1;
20      private Integer miningPoints = 0;
21      private Double luck = 0.0;
22
23      private ArrayList<Transaction> transactionLedger = new
        ArrayList<>();
```

The first thing we recognize on line 13 is that this class implements the interface `Serializable`. Since all the blocks for our blockchain will be created using this class, we need them to be serializable so that we can share our blockchain through our network.

The field `prevHash` will contain the signature or, in other words, the encrypted data from the previous block. The `currHash` will contain the signature or, in other words, the encrypted data from this block, which will be encrypted with the private key of the miner that will get to mine this block. The `timeStamp` obviously will contain a timestamp of when this block was mined/finalized. The field `minedBy` will contain the public key, which also doubles as the public address of the miner that managed to mine this block. In the process of blockchain verification, this public address/public key will be used to verify that the `currHash`/signature of this block is the same as the hash of the data presented by this block and secondary that this block was indeed mined by this particular miner.

We will touch on this topic a bit later in this section when we explain the isVerified method of this class. Next is our ledgerId field. Since we intend to implement a database with separate Block and Transaction tables, this field will help us retrieve the correct corresponding ledger for this block. You can also look at this field as the block number. Our next fields, miningPoints and luck, will be used to form the network consensus in regard to choosing this block's miner.

We will get into the details of how these fields are used in Chapter 6. The field transactionLedger is simply an arraylist of all the transactions contained in this block. We will explain the Transaction class in the section "Transaction.java."

In the following snippet, we can see the three constructors starting on line 26, line 38, and line 45:

```
25      //This constructor is used when we retrieve it
        from the db
26      public Block(byte[] prevHash, byte[] currHash,
         String timeStamp, byte[] minedBy,Integer ledgerId,
27           Integer miningPoints, Double luck,
              ArrayList<Transaction> transactionLedger) {
28          this.prevHash = prevHash;
29          this.currHash = currHash;
30          this.timeStamp = timeStamp;
31          this.minedBy = minedBy;
32          this.ledgerId = ledgerId;
33          this.transactionLedger = transactionLedger;
34          this.miningPoints = miningPoints;
35          this.luck = luck;
36      }
37      //This constructor is used when we initiate it after
        retrieve.
38      public Block(LinkedList<Block> currentBlockChain) {
```

```
39          Block lastBlock = currentBlockChain.getLast();
40          prevHash = lastBlock.getCurrHash();
41          ledgerId = lastBlock.getLedgerId() + 1;
42          luck = Math.random() * 1000000;
43      }
44      //This constructor is used only for creating the first
        block in the blockchain.
45      public Block() {
46          prevHash = new byte[]{0};
47      }
48
```

The first constructor is used when we retrieve our blockchain from the database. Here we retrieve all the blocks completely finalized, and this constructor helps us instantiate the block with all of the fields properly set up. The second constructor is used while the application is running and is used to create a completely new block (in other words, the head of the blockchain) for us to work on. We will go over the details of how this is achieved in Chapter 6. Our third constructor on line 45 will be used only once by our `init()` method to create our first block.

Our next snippet showcases the `isVerified` method:

```
48
49      public Boolean isVerified(Signature signing)
50              throws InvalidKeyException, SignatureException {
51          signing.initVerify(new DSAPublicKeyImpl(this.minedBy));
52          signing.update(this.toString().getBytes());
53          return signing.verify(this.currHash);
54      }
55
```

We accept an object from the Signature class as a parameter. The Signature class is actually a class from the java security package java.security.Signature. It is a helper singleton class that allows us to encrypt/decrypt data using different algorithms. On line 51 we initiate the signing parameter by using the public key from the minedBy field of this class. We will use this key to verify the data in this class against the signature stored in the currHash. On line 52 we insert the data that we want to verify, which in our case is the contents of the toString method. On line 53 we return the Boolean result after verifying the data contained in this class against its currHash.

What's left, as shown in our next snippet, are the equals and hash methods, the generic getters and setters, and the toString() method, which concludes our Block.java class:

```
55
56      @Override
57      public boolean equals(Object o) {
58          if (this == o) return true;
59          if (!(o instanceof Block)) return false;
60          Block block = (Block) o;
61          return Arrays.equals(getPrevHash(),
            block.getPrevHash());
62      }
63
64      @Override
65      public int hashCode() {
66          return Arrays.hashCode(getPrevHash());
67      }
68
69      public byte[] getPrevHash() { return prevHash; }
70      public byte[] getCurrHash() { return currHash; }
71
```

```
72      public void setPrevHash(byte[] prevHash) { this.prevHash =
        prevHash; }
73      public void setCurrHash(byte[] currHash) { this.currHash =
        currHash; }
74
75      public ArrayList<Transaction> getTransactionLedger() {
        return transactionLedger; }
76      public void setTransactionLedger(
            ArrayList<Transaction> transactionLedger) {
77              this.transactionLedger = transactionLedger;
78      }
79
80      public String getTimeStamp() { return timeStamp; }
81      public void setMinedBy(byte[] minedBy) {
                this.minedBy = minedBy; }
82
83      public void setTimeStamp(String timeStamp) {
                this.timeStamp = timeStamp; }
84
85      public byte[] getMinedBy() { return minedBy; }
86
87      public Integer getMiningPoints() { return miningPoints; }
88      public void setMiningPoints(Integer miningPoints) {
                this.miningPoints = miningPoints; }
89      public Double getLuck() { return luck; }
90      public void setLuck(Double luck) { this.luck = luck; }
91
92      public Integer getLedgerId() { return ledgerId; }
93      public void setLedgerId(Integer ledgerId) {
                this.ledgerId = ledgerId; }
94
```

```
95      @Override
96      public String toString() {
97          return "Block{" +
98                  "prevHash=" + Arrays.toString(prevHash) +
99                  ", timeStamp='" + timeStamp + '\'' +
100                 ", minedBy=" + Arrays.toString(minedBy) +
101                 ", ledgerId=" + ledgerId +
102                 ", miningPoints=" + miningPoints +
103                 ", luck=" + luck +
104                 '}';
105     }
106}
107
```

The first thing to note here is that the `equals` method compares the previous hash of the block class. We'll use this later in Chapter 6 when we explain the consensus algorithm further. The other thing of note is the fields contained in the `toString` method. We include everything that goes into verifying the block against the current hash.

Important!

- Remember that a wallet's public key is also the wallet's public address/account number.
- The current hash/signature of the block is just the encrypted version of the data contained in the block.
- The miner's private key is used to encrypt the block's data, which creates the signature.

- The miner's public key is used for other peers to verify the block by comparing the signature's hash against the hash of the block's data.
- Note how we use the `toString()` method throughout this class to prep our data conveniently for comparison.
- Note how all of the essential fields that make certain the block is unique are included in the `toString()` method.

2.2 Transaction.java

We briefly mentioned that we keep an array list of transactions in our `Block` class in the previous section, and now it's time to explain in detail what our `Transaction.java` class contains. First we'll start with the imports found in the following code snippet:

```
1  package com.company.Model;
2
3  import sun.security.provider.DSAPublicKeyImpl;
4
5  import java.io.Serializable;
6  import java.security.InvalidKeyException;
7  import java.security.Signature;
8  import java.security.SignatureException;
9  import java.time.LocalDateTime;
10 import java.util.Arrays;
11 import java.util.Base64;
12
```

Next let's go over the class declaration and its fields, as shown in the next code snippet:

```
13 public class Transaction implements Serializable {
14
15     private byte[] from;
16     private String fromFX;
17     private byte[] to;
18     private String toFX;
19     private Integer value;
20     private String timestamp;
21     private byte[] signature;
22     private String signatureFX;
23     private Integer ledgerId;
24
```

Since this class also creates objects from which we are building our blockchain, it will implement the interface serializable so that it's shareable through the network.

The fields `from` and `to` will contain the public keys/addresses of the account that sends and the account that receives the coins, respectively. The value is the amount of coins that will be sent, and `timeStamp` is the time at which the transaction has occurred. `Signature` will contain the encrypted information of all the fields, and it will be used to verify the validity of the transaction (it will be used the same way the field `currHash` was used in the previous class).The `ledgerId` serves the same purpose as in the previous class. The fields with the `FX` suffix are simple duplicates formatted to `String` instead of `byte[]`. We do this so that we can easily display them on our front end.

In this class we also have two constructors; the first one is used when we retrieve a transaction from the database, and the second one is used when we want to create a new transaction within our application. Let's observe them in the following code snippet:

```
26    //Constructor for loading with existing signature
27    public Transaction(byte[] from, byte[] to, Integer value,
      byte[] signature, Integer ledgerId,
28                          String timeStamp) {
29       Base64.Encoder encoder = Base64.getEncoder();
30       this.from = from;
31       this.fromFX = encoder.encodeToString(from);
32       this.to = to;
33       this.toFX = encoder.encodeToString(to);
34       this.value = value;
35       this.signature = signature;
36       this.signatureFX = encoder.encodeToString(signature);
37       this.ledgerId = ledgerId;
38       this.timestamp = timeStamp;
39    }
40    //Constructor for creating a new transaction and
      signing it.
41    public Transaction (Wallet fromWallet, byte[] toAddress,
      Integer value, Integer ledgerId,
42                          Signature signing) throws
                  InvalidKeyException, SignatureException {
43       Base64.Encoder encoder = Base64.getEncoder();
44       this.from = fromWallet.getPublicKey().getEncoded();
45       this.fromFX = encoder.encodeToString(
         fromWallet.getPublicKey().getEncoded());
46       this.to = toAddress;
47       this.toFX = encoder.encodeToString(toAddress);
48       this.value = value;
49       this.ledgerId = ledgerId;
50       this.timestamp = LocalDateTime.now().toString();
51       signing.initSign(fromWallet.getPrivateKey());
```

```
52          String sr = this.toString();
53          signing.update(sr.getBytes());
54          this.signature = signing.sign();
55          this.signatureFX = encoder.encodeToString(this
            .signature);
56      }
57
```

The first constructor simply sets the class fields according to the retrieved data from the database and uses the `Base64.Encoder` class to convert the `byte[]` fields safely into `String`.

The second constructor is a bit more complex, so we will explain it in more detail piece by piece. First let's look at the constructor parameters that are different: `Wallet fromWallet` and `Signature signing`. We will explain the `Wallet` class in more detail in the next section, for now we should just note that the `fromWallet` parameter contains the public and private keys of the sender/maker of the transaction. We use the same `Signature` class as in our `Block isVerified` method mentioned in the previous section.

Next let's explain the body of the constructor so we understand how encrypting data works in our case. The signature creation phase shown in Figure 2-1 offers an overview of what we are trying to accomplish.

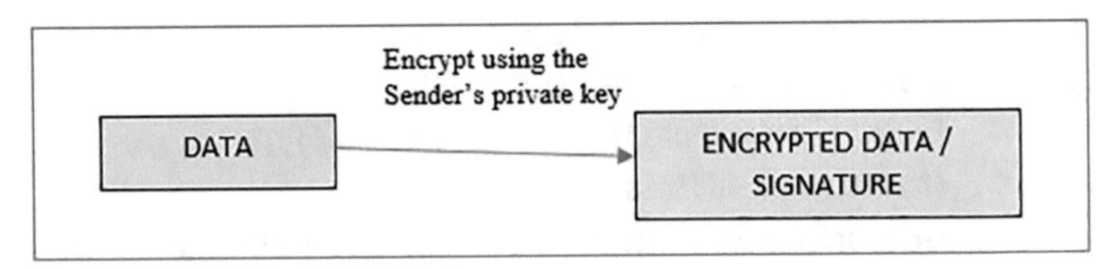

Figure 2-1. *Signature creation*

To achieve this, first we set up our data by initiating our class fields from the parameters and add a timestamp as shown on lines 44 to 50. Now once we have our data that we would like to encrypt, we set our private key to the signing object with the statement on line 51. This tells the signing object, when encrypting, to use the private key we provided. On line 52 we are putting all the data we want to encrypt in a single String object by using the toString() method. On line 53 we are feeding all the data we want to encrypt to the signing object, and on line 54 we are actually encrypting the data and assigning it to our signature field.

Next is our method for the verification of transactions, as shown in the following snippet:

```
58    public Boolean isVerified(Signature signing)
59            throws InvalidKeyException, SignatureException {
60        signing.initVerify(new DSAPublicKeyImpl(this.
          getFrom()));
61        signing.update(this.toString().getBytes());
62        return signing.verify(this.signature);
63    }
64
```

This method will be used by the other peers to verify that each transaction is valid. Before explaining the code, let's look at Figure 2-2 and see what our method tries to accomplish.

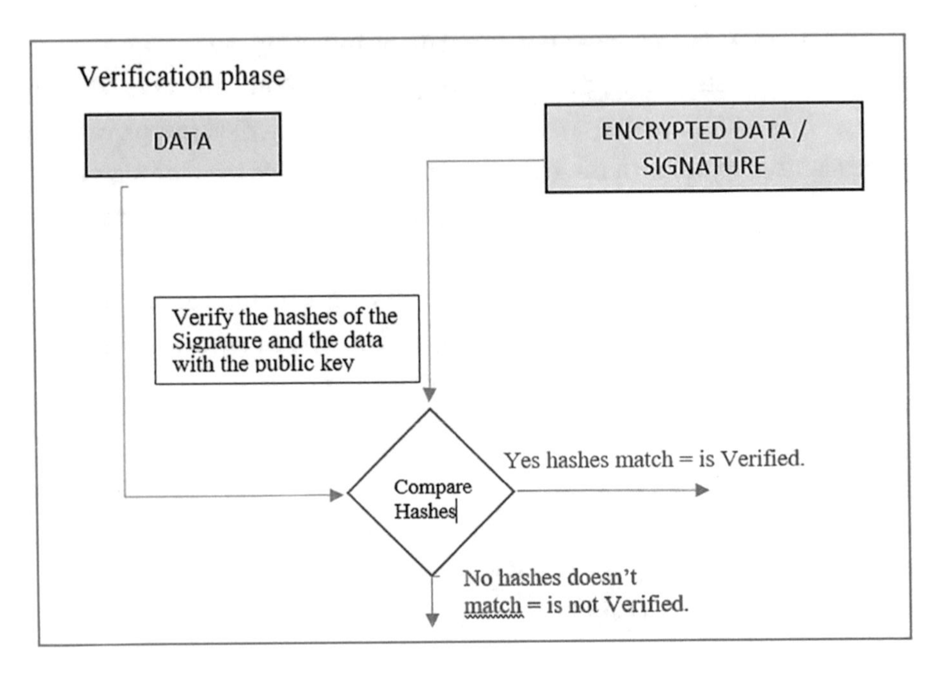

Figure 2-2. *Verification phase*

The workflow of the schematic is quite simple; we need to compare the hash of the signature and the hash of the data contained in our class using the public key.

Now let's look back at our `isVerified` method and explain how the workflow from the schematic is achieved. As parameters we are getting the `Transaction` object that we want to verify and the `Signature` helper class object, which pre-initialized to use SHA256 with DSA algorithm the same way as before. On line 60 we are setting the public key with which we would like to decrypt our signature. The new `DSAPublicKeyImpl(byte[] encoded)` is just a wrapper from the `sun.security.provider` package that will help convert our public key information from `byte[]` to `PublicKey` object. On line 61 we set the transaction data that we want to verify against the signature. Finally on line Blockchaintransaction.java 62 we provide the signature, the process of comparison/verification gets executed and a result is returned automatically for us.

We finish up the rest of the class with generic getters, setters, and our toString, equals, and hash methods, as shown in the following snippet:

```
65    @Override
66    public String toString() {
67       return "Transaction{" +
68                "from=" + Arrays.toString(from) +
69                ", to=" + Arrays.toString(to) +
70                ", value=" + value +
71                ", timeStamp= " + timestamp +
72                ", ledgerId=" + ledgerId +
73                '}';
74    }
75
76    public byte[] getFrom() { return from; }
77    public void setFrom(byte[] from) { this.from = from; }
78
79    public byte[] getTo() { return to; }
80    public void setTo(byte[] to) { this.to = to; }
81
82    public Integer getValue() { return value; }
83    public void setValue(Integer value) { this.value = value; }
84    public byte[] getSignature() { return signature; }
85
86    public Integer getLedgerId() { return ledgerId; }
87    public void setLedgerId(Integer ledgerId) {
      this.ledgerId = ledgerId; }
88
89    public String getTimestamp() { return timestamp; }
90
91    public String getFromFX() { return fromFX; }
92    public String getToFX() { return toFX; }
```

```
93     public String getSignatureFX() { return signatureFX; }
94
95
96     @Override
97     public boolean equals(Object o) {
98         if (this == o) return true;
99         if (!(o instanceof Transaction)) return false;
100        Transaction that = (Transaction) o;
101        return Arrays.equals(getSignature(),
           that.getSignature());
102    }
103
104    @Override
105    public int hashCode() {
106        return Arrays.hashCode(getSignature());
107    }
108
109}
```

Important!

- Note how we use the `toString()` method throughout this class to prep our data conveniently for comparison.
- Note how all the essential fields that make certain the transaction is unique are included in the `toString()` method.

EXERCISE 2-1

If we fail to include a timestamp as part of the verification process in our transaction object, can you think of a way to exploit this vulnerability?

2.3 Wallet.java

Let's start as always with the imports for this class located in the following snippet:

```
1 package com.company.Model;
2
3 import java.io.Serializable;
4 import java.security.*;
5
```

In the following snippet, observe the class declaration and fields:

```
6 public class Wallet implements Serializable {
7
8     private KeyPair keyPair;
9
```

Since we would like to be able to store and export/import our wallet from/to a database, we will also implement the `Serializable` interface. This class will contain a single field that will be an object of the `KeyPair` class. This class is part of the `java.security` package and contains the public key and private key that we mentioned in the previous sections.

Important!

- Note how our blockchain wallet doesn't require any information regarding the wallet holder. This is the basis of the wallet holder's anonymity.
- Our blockchain wallet also won't contain any field containing the current balance of the wallet. We will explain how we obtain our wallet balance in Chapter 6.

Let's look at our first two constructors on our next snippet, which will be used when we want to create a new wallet and assign a new key pair to it:

```
10      //Constructors for generating new KeyPair
11      public Wallet() throws NoSuchAlgorithmException {
12          this(2048, KeyPairGenerator.getInstance("DSA"));
13      }
14      public Wallet(Integer keySize, KeyPairGenerator
        keyPairGen) {
15          keyPairGen.initialize(keySize);
16          this.keyPair = keyPairGen.generateKeyPair();
17      }
```

The first no parameters constructor will call the second constructor with a default keySize and a KeyPairGenerator instance set to generate keys using the DSA algorithm. The second constructor receives these input parameters either from the first or from other parts of the application and simply sets the size of the keys on line 15 and generates the keys themselves on line 16.

Our third constructor will be used to create our wallet once we have imported an already existing key pair from our database. We can observe it in the following snippet:

```
18
19     //Constructor for importing Keys only
20     public Wallet(PublicKey publicKey, PrivateKey privateKey) {
21         this.keyPair = new KeyPair(publicKey,privateKey);
22     }
```

The code here simply receives public and private key objects and creates a new KeyPair object with them.

Finally, we finish up this class and chapter by including the generic getters and setters in the following snippet:

```
23
24     public KeyPair getKeyPair() { return keyPair; }
25
26     public PublicKey getPublicKey() { return
       keyPair.getPublic(); }
27     public PrivateKey getPrivateKey() {
               return keyPair.getPrivate(); }
28}
```

2.4 Summary

In this chapter, we covered the creation of our model layer of the application. These classes and their methods will be used as basic building blocks throughout the rest of the application. Therefore, having nice grasp of them now will greatly benefit you in understanding the more complex logic in the upcoming chapters. This is a small recap of what concepts we covered so far:

- Representation of a single block of the blockchain by implementing our `Block.java` class
- Java implementation of importing blocks from an existing blockchain and creation of the head block of the blockchain
- Representation of a blockchain transaction by implementing our `Transaction.java` class
- Java implementation for importing transactions and creating new transactions
- Java implementation of encryption and verification (creating signatures and verifying them)
- Representation of a blockchain wallet by implementing our `Wallet.java` class

Answer to Exercise 2-1: Someone can copy and paste a signed transaction, and it will pass the validation checks since there is no way to make sure the transaction is unique in time.

CHAPTER 3

Database Setup

"Blocks Database" by Filip Rizov

S. Buzharovski, *Introducing Blockchain with Java*,
https://doi.org/10.1007/978-1-4842-7927-4_3

For a greater visualization of our blockchain and our wallet data, we chose to implement a SQLite database instead of storing it in raw file data format. Our plan is to set up one database for our blockchain and another for our wallet just so we can maintain better separation of concerns and increase security. In this chapter, we will learn how to set up our databases from scratch and write an `init()` method for our application that will write our table schemas in SQL with preset defaults. For this purpose we will be using the SQLite JDBC driver and SQLite database browser.

3.1 SQLite Database Browser Setup

First we will be downloading our SQLite database browser from `https://sqlitebrowser.org/dl/`. Just download the recommended version for your operating system and install it on your machine with the recommended settings. Once you run it, the app should look something like Figure 3-1.

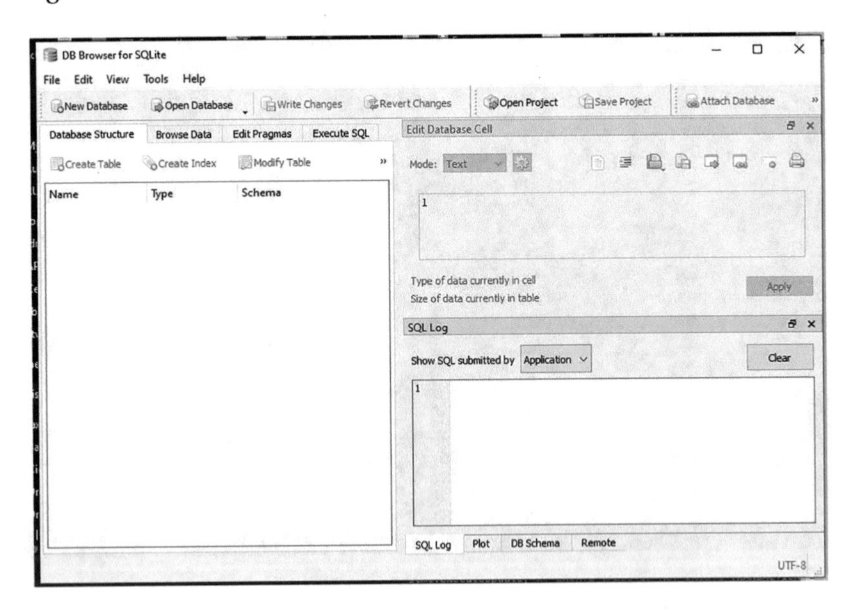

Figure 3-1. *Our app*

This means that you have installed the database browser successfully, and we can move on to setting up our actual databases.

3.2 Blockchain.db

Our first database that we will implement is the one for storing our blockchain data, and we will name it appropriately as `blockchain.db`. In this chapter, we will learn to set up our database step-by-step by using the SQLite browser. However, in the section "Writing your App init() Method," we will learn to set up our database programmatically by using SQL and SQL JDBC driver. Ideally this chapter will go a long way in visualizing the data contained in the blockchain through the database browser and help bridge the gap for people less familiar with SQL. The "Writing your App init() Method" section will give you the SQL code and teach you how to programmatically implement your database setup in the future.

We start by clicking the New Database button New Database or go to File and then click the New Database command in case the button tray doesn't show. This should open a screen similar to Figure 3-2, asking us to name our database and choose a filepath for saving it.

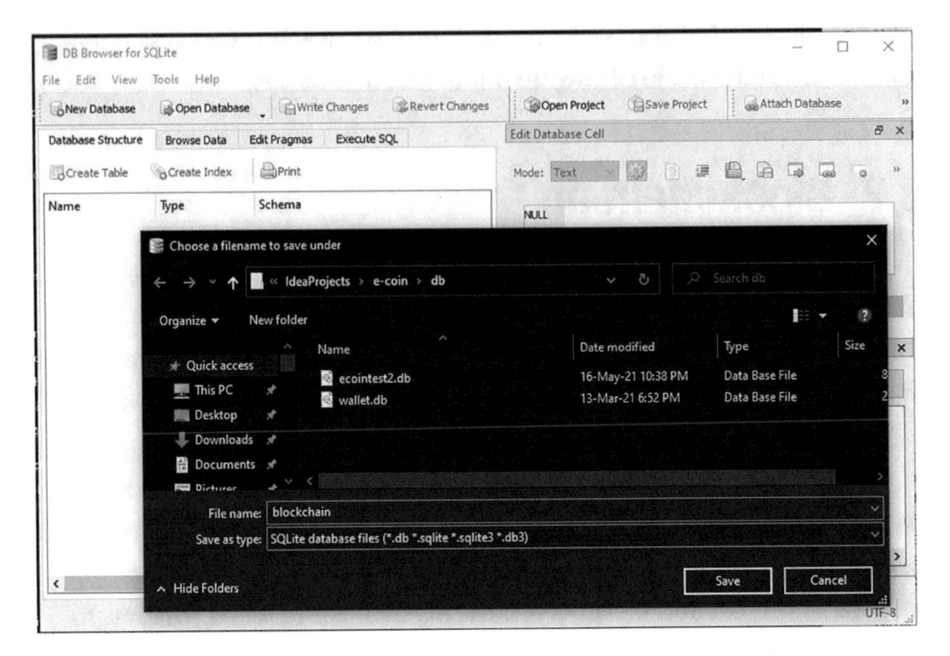

Figure 3-2. *Naming and saving our database*

I chose to create a folder named `db` in my `e-coin` project folder and name the database `blockchain`. You can choose a different name or location for your database; just make sure you remember to use those names throughout instead of the ones in this book's instructions. Once we click Save, we are greeted with the window shown in Figure 3-3 that prompts us to create our first table.

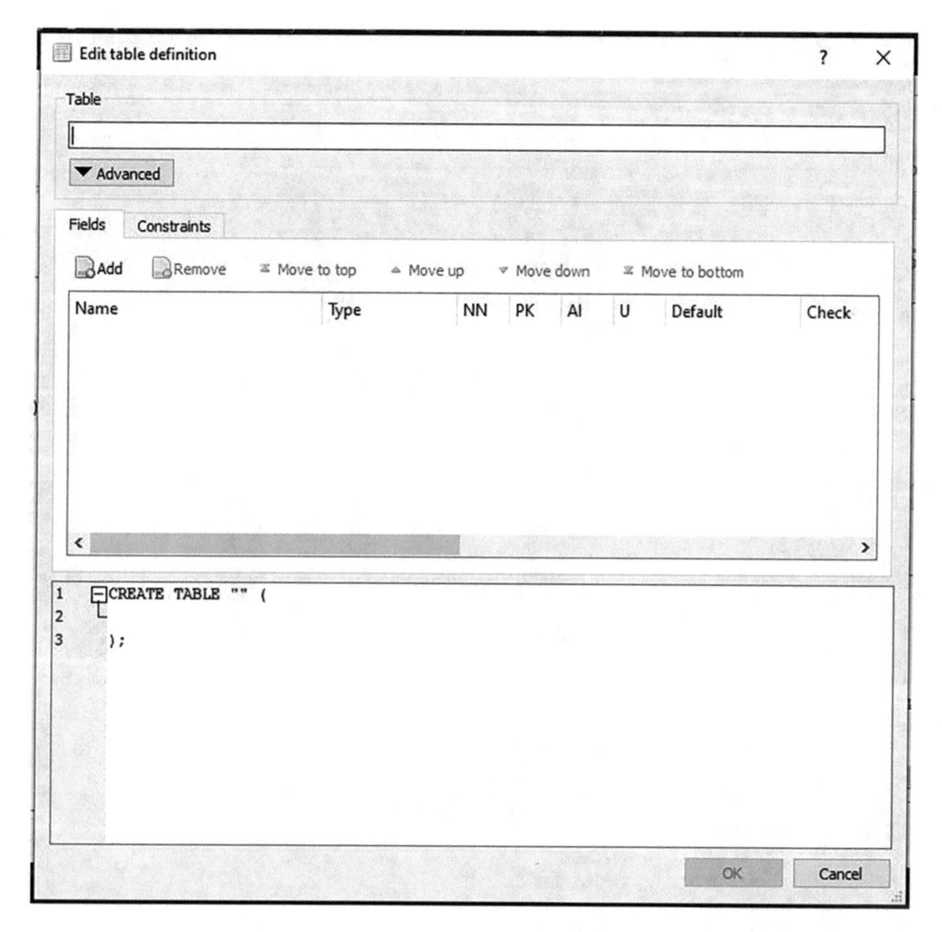

Figure 3-3. *Creating a table*

We will name our table BLOCKCHAIN, and we want it to store all of our blocks and the data they contain. Now in the upper window on the tab named Fields, we will click the Add button to add a field row. These field rows will represent the table columns, so from now on we will refer to them as such. When you start creating your columns in the upper window, you will notice that the SQL code in the lower window will modify itself to correspond to your choices. For now let's look at Figure 3-4 and set up our table columns accordingly.

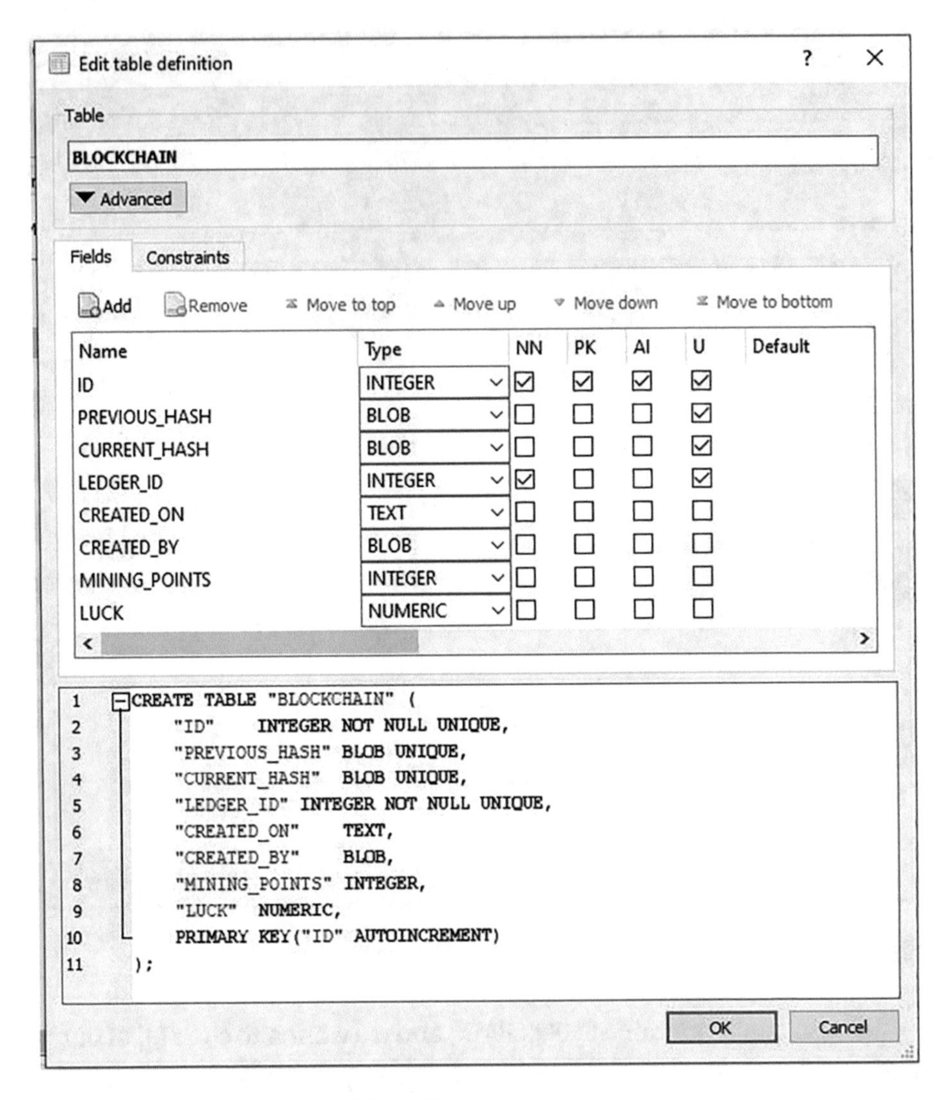

Figure 3-4. *Setting up table columns*

If you noticed that the names of the columns are similar to the names of the fields of the `Block.java` class, then great job; having a different column for each class field is exactly how we want to store our data. Each row in our `BLOCKCHAIN` table will represent a different block, so we also include an `ID` column here, which will number our blocks. The type chosen for our column corresponds closely to the types of the fields in the `Block.java` class in order to maintain the integrity of the data. This is especially important for all our class fields of the byte array type to be stored as `BLOB`; otherwise, the conversion to another type will change the original information and render the public keys and signatures stored in them invalid. You can read up more on SQLite types if you are interested at `https://www.w3resource.com/sqlite/sqlite-data-types.php`. Now once we click the OK button, we will have our first table in our database created, and our database browser should look like Figure 3-5.

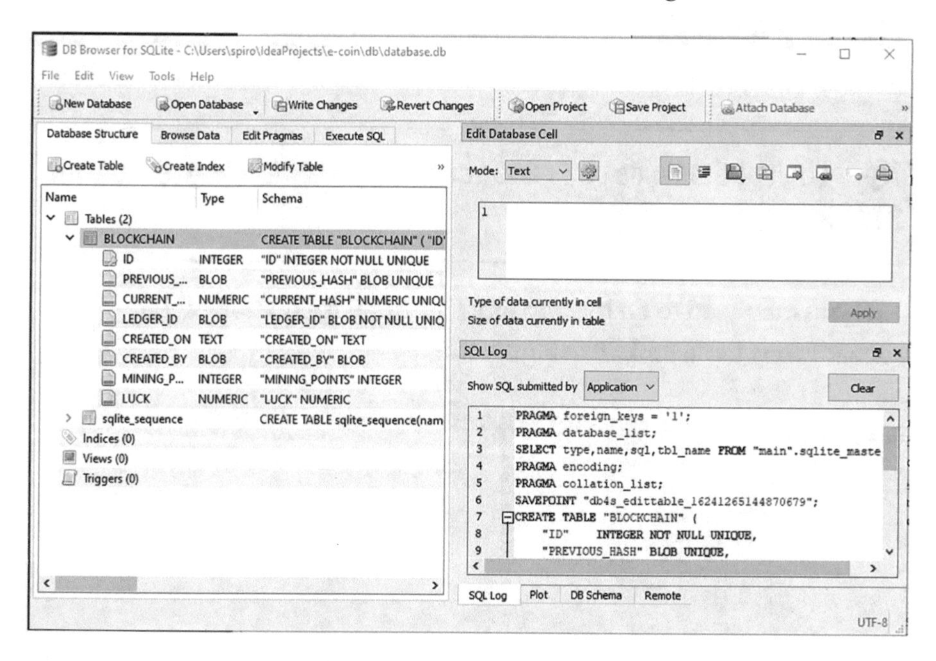

***Figure 3-5.** Our first table in our database*

Our next step is to create a table that will contain the transactions included in each block. For that purpose we click the Create Table button and get another window looking exactly like the window we used to create our BLOCKCHAIN table.

EXERCISE 3-1

Try creating the next table named TRANSACTIONS on your own before learning how we did it.

Tip Look at the fields of `Transaction.java` just like we did with `Block.java`.

If you managed to do it, good job! Our implementation of the `Transactions` table looks like Figure 3-6.

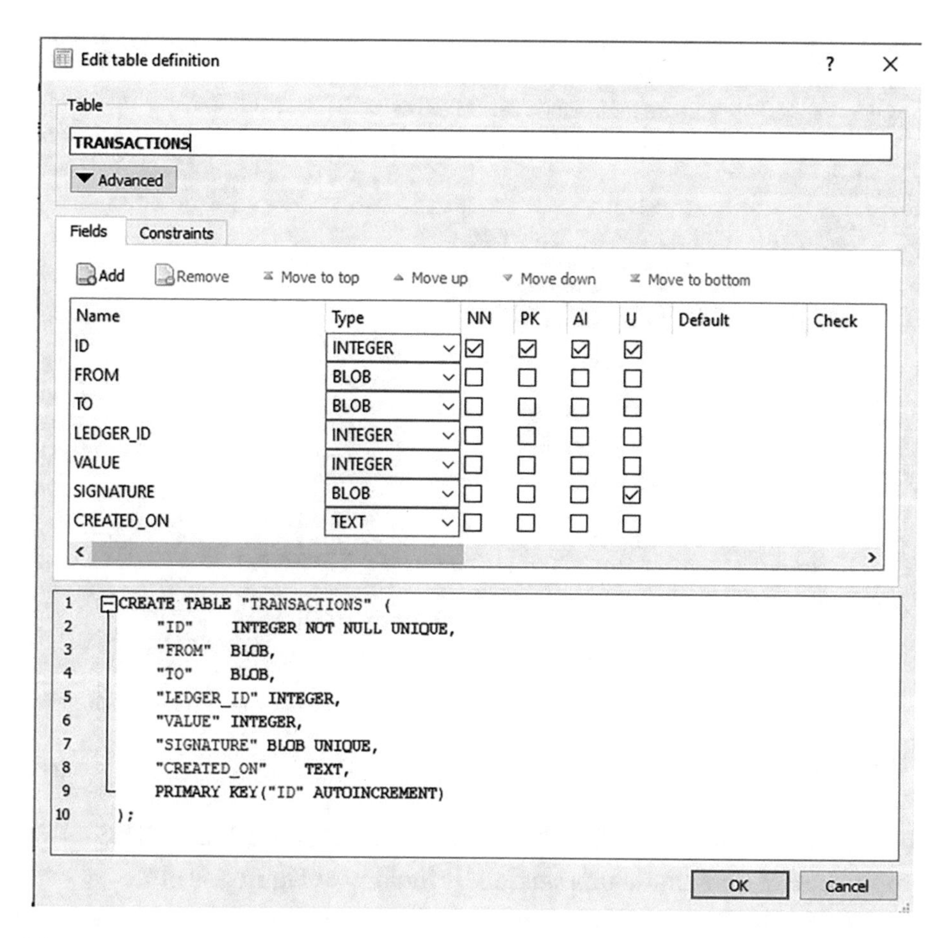

Figure 3-6. *Transactions table*

Finally, the complete database schema should look like Figure 3-7.

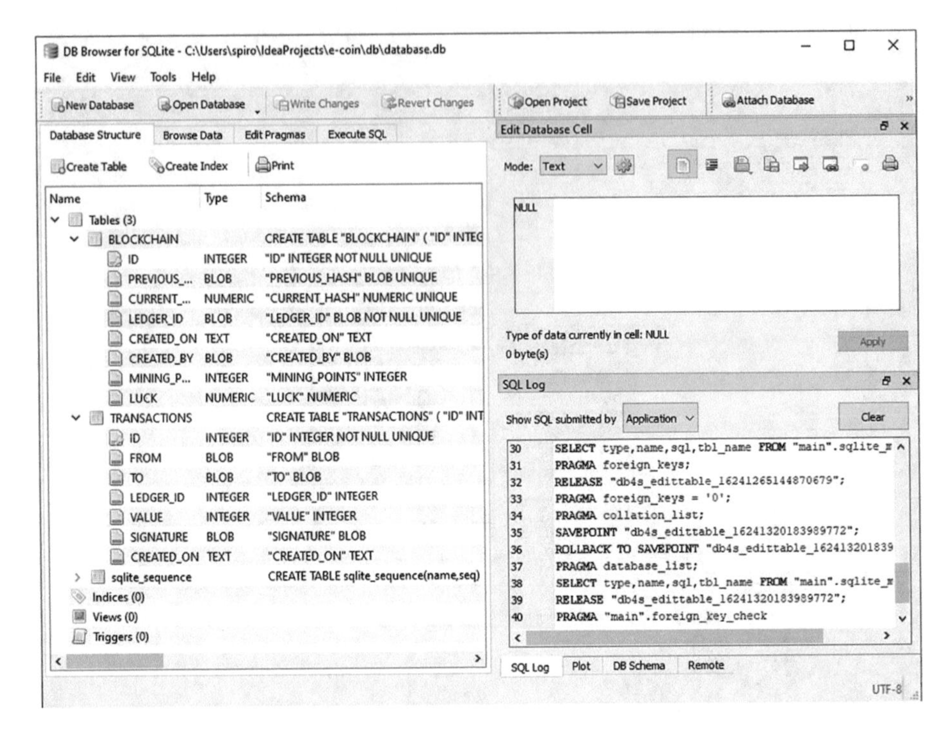

Figure 3-7. *Complete database schema*

Now obviously if you click the Browse Data tab, the tables will be empty, but let's conclude this section by looking at Figure 3-8 and Figure 3-9, which contain some dummy data so we can visualize how everything will fall into place once we complete the rest of our application.

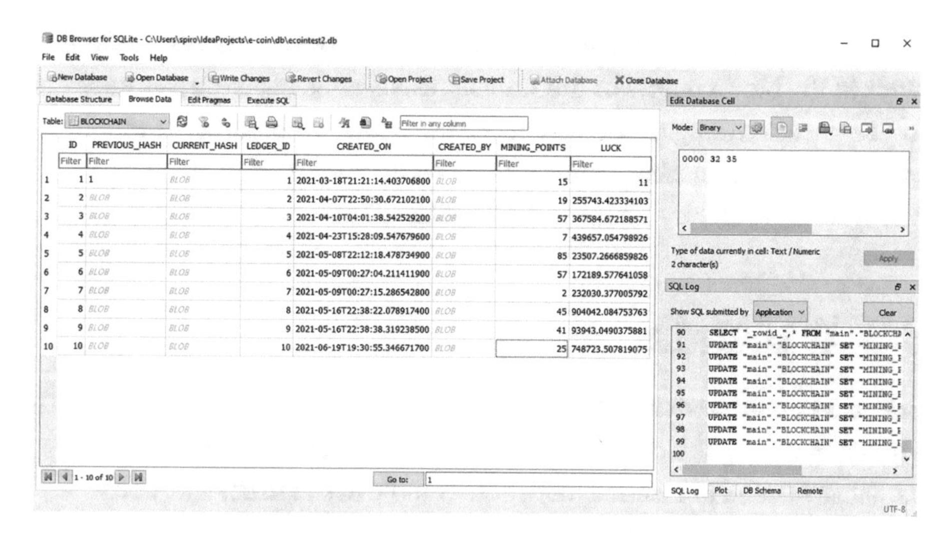

Figure 3-8. *BLOCKCHAIN table with dummy data*

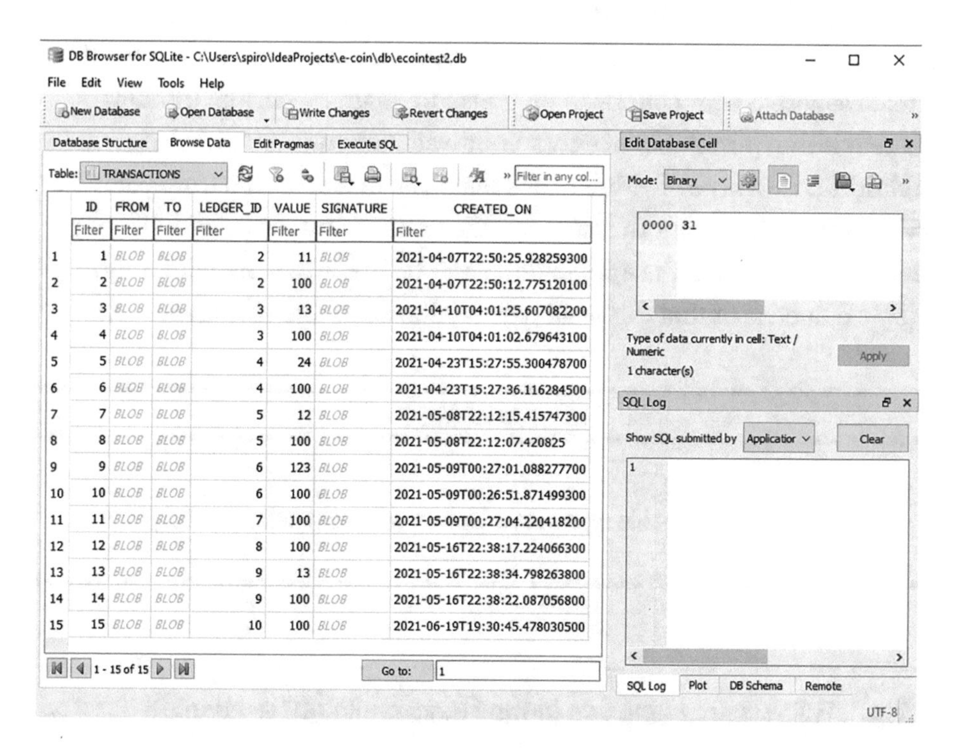

Figure 3-9. *Transaction table with dummy data*

For the BLOCKCHAIN table in Figure 3-8, each row represents a different block in the blockchain. For the Transactions table in Figure 3-9, each row represents a single transaction. All transactions containing the same LEDGER_ID number represent transactions contained in a single corresponding block with the same LEDGER_ID number.

3.3 Wallet.db

Before we go through basically the same steps for creating Wallet.db, let's explain our design decision as to why we create the wallet in a separate database instead of creating just another table in our blockchain.db database. It's because this way we get a clear separation of concerns. All the data in the blockchain database is supposed to get shared over a peer-to-peer network, and all the data in your Wallet.db database is supposed to be kept away from others; therefore, having your application create separate connections to both also increases security. Another benefit is that portability of either your wallet or your blockchain is just a simple copy/paste of either blockchain.db or wallet.db from your current machine to another without the need of any extra code. Of course, this is not to say that the application can't be made to work with only a single database or that this is all you need to keep everything secure.

EXERCISE 3-2

Try creating the next table named WALLET on your own before looking how we did it.

Tip Follow same steps as in the "Blockchain.db" section.

If you managed to do it and realize that we might need to split the keyPair field in our Wallet.java class into two columns, one for each key, then great job. If not, then let's go over the steps again. Let's click the New Database button, name our table WALLET, and in it create two columns called PRIVATE_KEY and PUBLIC_KEY that will constitute our keypair. It should look similar to Figure 3-10.

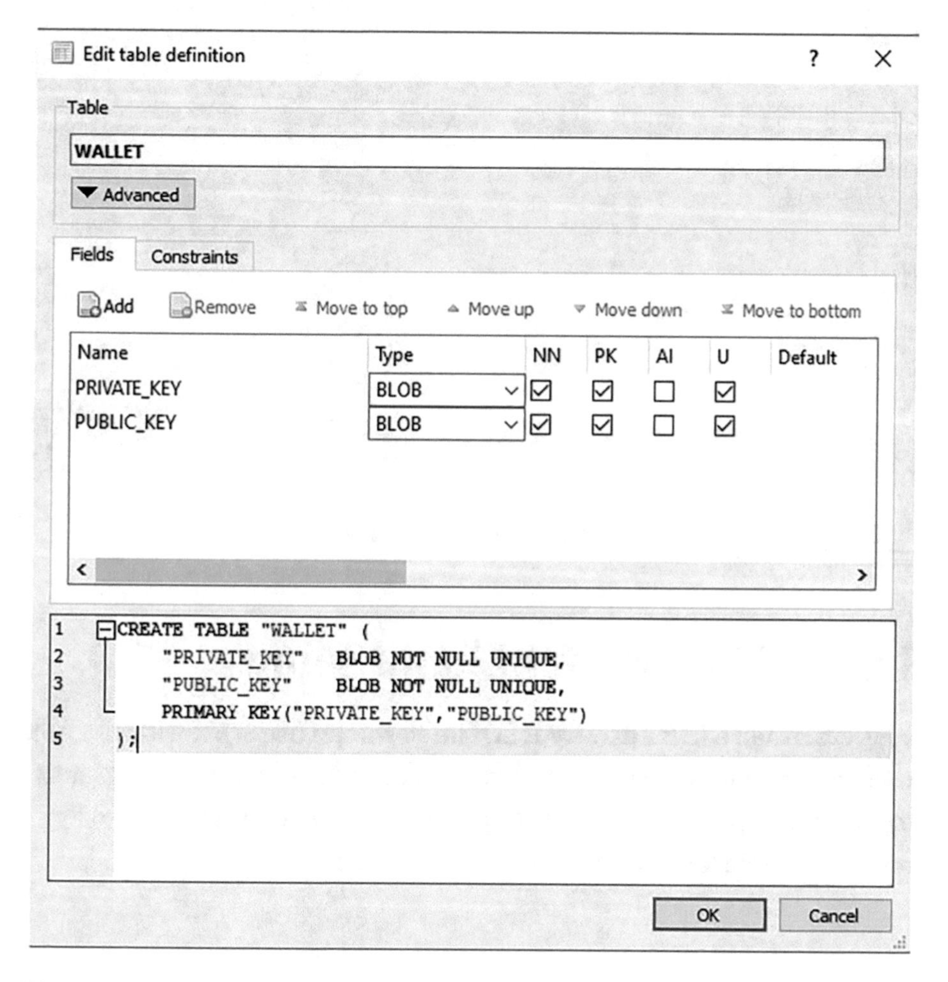

Figure 3-10. *Creating our keypair*

Our complete database schema for our `wallet.db` database will look like Figure 3-11.

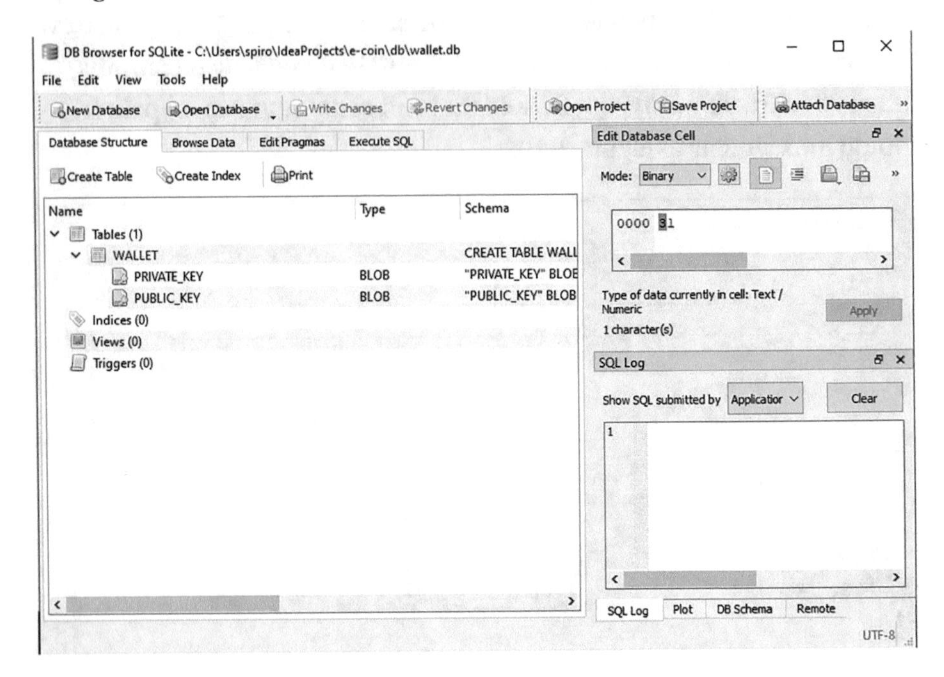

Figure 3-11. *Database schema for wallet.db*

3.4 JDBC Driver for SQLite Setup

Now let's install a JDBC driver for SQLite so we can use SQL inside our app to set up the same schemas. Visit `https://search.maven.org/artifact/org.xerial/sqlite-jdbc/3.34.0/jar` and download the JAR manually from the downloads option, as shown in Figure 3-11.

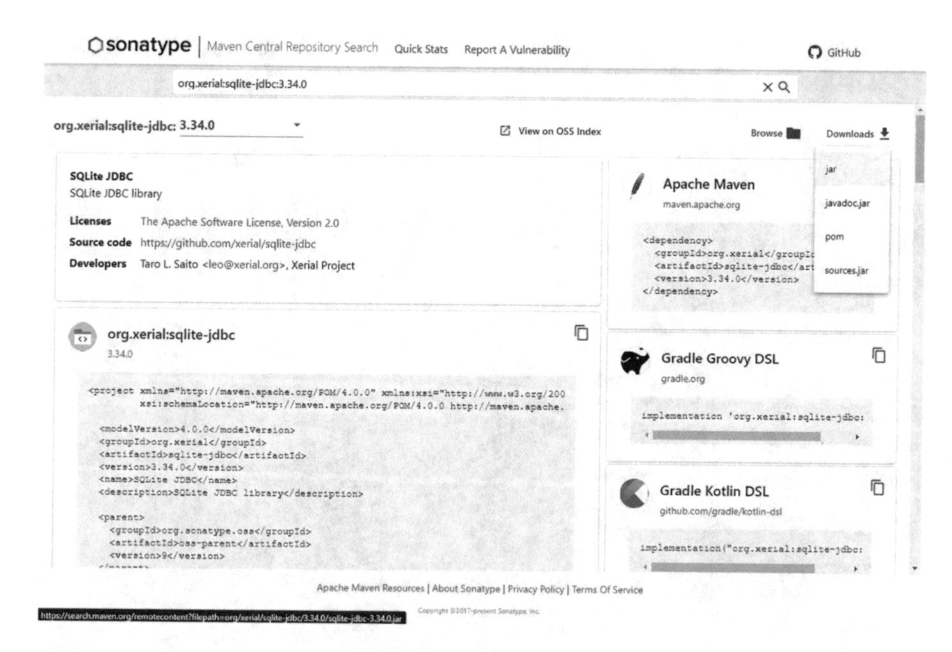

Figure 3-12. *Downloading JARs*

You can create a `libs` folder inside your project folder and save it there just like we have in our repository. Next Select File and then Project Structure; then go to the Libraries tab in Project Settings, click the plus sign to add new project library, choose Java, and select the JAR file we just downloaded then click OK. Look at Figures 3-13 and 3-14 for visual help.

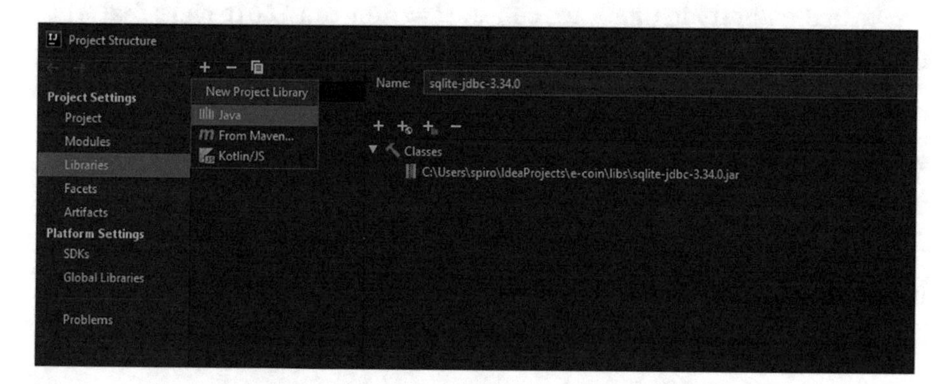

Figure 3-13. *Selecting Java*

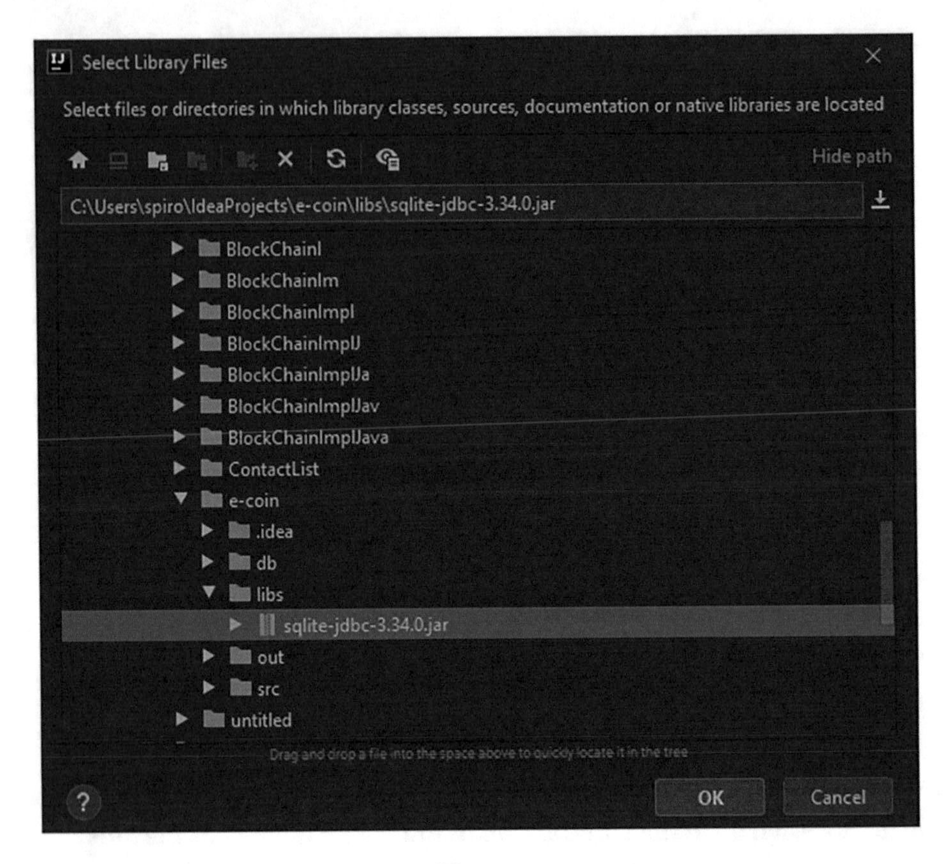

Figure 3-14. *Selecting the JAR file*

With the library in place, we can start writing our `ECoin` class that will contain our `main` and `init()` methods.

3.5 Writing Your App init() Method

Let's briefly start with looking at our `ECoin.java` class before we jump inside its `init()` method. Our `ECoin.java` class is located in the `src.com.company` folder structure in our repository. This is our main application class; in other words, our application starts from here. Our next snippet shows the class imports, class declaration, the main method, and the start method:

```
1  package com.company;
2
3  import com.company.Model.Block;
4  import com.company.Model.Transaction;
5  import com.company.Model.Wallet;
6  import com.company.ServiceData.BlockchainData;
7  import com.company.ServiceData.WalletData;
8  import com.company.Threads.MiningThread;
9  import com.company.Threads.PeerClient;
10 import com.company.Threads.PeerServer;
11 import com.company.Threads.UI;
12 import javafx.application.Application;
13 import javafx.stage.Stage;
14
15 import java.security.*;
16 import java.sql.*;
17 import java.time.LocalDateTime;
18
19 public class ECoin extends Application {
20
21     public static void main(String[] args) {
22         launch(args);
23     }
24
25     @Override
26     public void start(Stage primaryStage) throws Exception {
27         new UI().start(primaryStage);
28         new PeerClient().start();
```

```
29            new PeerServer(6000).start();
30            new MiningThread().start();
31        }
32
```

On line 19 we can see that our class extends the Application class. Application is part of the jaxafx package, and by extending it we show that we will be running our application as a javafx application. Since the Application class is actually an abstract class, by extending it we need to implement the start(Stage s) method before we can run our app. On lines 26 to 31 you can see our implementation of the start(Stage s) method. Each line of the method body (lines 27–30) represents a different thread that will run in parallel in our application. The thread on line 27 will display our UI and execute commands associated with it. The thread on line 28 will act as a client and query other peers. The thread on line 29 will act as a server and respond to incoming queries from other peers. The thread on line 30 will run the blockchain verification and consensus tasks continuously. We will talk about each thread in our future sections and explain how each thread works in detail. For now the explanation of what these threads are trying to accomplish is enough and should give you a nice overview of how our application is structured when it comes to the topic of what it tries to accomplish.

It's finally time to talk about our init() method and what we will accomplish with it. The init() method runs before our application start(Stage s) method, and its purpose is to check and set up the necessary prerequisites so that our application can run. In our case, those prerequisites include the existence of our wallet.db and blockchain.db, their schemas, and their contents. Let's look at the following snippet and start explaining the code:

```
32
33        @Override
34        public void init() {
```

```
35          try {
36  //This creates your wallet if there is none and gives you a
    KeyPair.
37  //We will create it in separate db for better security and
    ease of portability.
38              Connection walletConnection = DriverManager
39                      .getConnection("jdbc:sqlite:C:\\Users\\
                        spiro\\IdeaProjects\\e-coin\\db\\
                        wallet.db");
40              Statement walletStatment =
                   walletConnection.createStatement();
41              walletStatment.executeUpdate("CREATE TABLE IF
                NOT EXISTS WALLET ( " +
42                      " PRIVATE_KEY BLOB NOT NULL UNIQUE, " +
43                      " PUBLIC_KEY BLOB NOT NULL UNIQUE, " +
44                      " PRIMARY KEY (PRIVATE_KEY, PUBLIC_KEY)" +
45                      ") "
46              );
47              ResultSet resultSet = walletStatment.execute
                Query(" SELECT * FROM WALLET ");
48              if (!resultSet.next()) {
49                  Wallet newWallet = new Wallet();
50                  byte[] pubBlob =
                     newWallet.getPublicKey().getEncoded();
51                  byte[] prvBlob =
                     newWallet.getPrivateKey().getEncoded();
52                  PreparedStatement pstmt = walletConnection
53                          .prepareStatement("INSERT INTO
                                WALLET(PRIVATE_KEY,
                                PUBLIC_KEY) " +
54                          " VALUES (?,?) ");
```

```
55                      pstmt.setBytes(1, prvBlob);
56                      pstmt.setBytes(2, pubBlob);
57                      pstmt.executeUpdate();
58                  }
59                  resultSet.close();
60                  walletStatment.close();
61                  walletConnection.close();
62                  WalletData.getInstance().loadWallet();
63
```

Line 38 and line 39 represent a single statement that uses our previously set-up SQLDriver to open a connection to our `wallet.db` database. The SQLDriver will check the existence of the `wallet.db` file in the provided URL location and open a connection to it. In case the file is missing, the SQLDriver will automatically create an empty `wallet.db` file.

On line 40 we use our established connection to the `wallet.db` database to instantiate our `Statement` object. Every time we use this `Statement` object to execute queries, it will execute them in the database that the connection that was used to instantiate it points at. In this case, that's `wallet.db`. On lines 41 to 46 we use the `executeUpdate(String s)` method on the `Statement` object named `walletStatment`, which takes `String` and executes it as SQL inside the `wallet.db`. The SQL string, except for the `IF NOT EXISTS` part that's added here, is identical to the SQL generated when we created the `WALLET` table manually, as shown in Figure 3-10. In other words, what our SQL here is saying is that if the `WALLET` table doesn't exist, create it with a schema identical to the one we created manually in the "Wallet.db" section.

In the next lines of code, lines 47–58, we will expand upon the functionality of our app to also recognize whether we have an existing keypair in our `wallet.db`. If it's empty, the app will generate a new keypair and populate our `WALLET` table with it. Line 47 queries the `WALLET` table and saves the results in the `ResultSet` object. Line 48 checks if the `resultSet` object is empty, and if it is, then lines 49–57 create a new wallet and export its keys to our Wallet table. Let's see what this set of functionalities allows us to do. We can run the app without any wallet.db, and it will automatically set up the database for it and create a new wallet for us. We can port our wallet to another machine by simply copying our wallet.db and replacing the wallet.db file on that machine. Our init() method will recognize that a keypair is present and won't try to overwrite it. The last thing to note is line 65. Here we will load the contents from our wallet.db into our WalletData singleton class. This will store our wallet data into the app memory and make it more readily accessible throughout the rest of our app. We will talk more about the WalletData class in our next chapter.

Now let's look at the next part of our init() method in the following snippet:

```
64 // This will create the db tables with columns for
   theBlockchain.
65     Connection blockchainConnection = DriverManager
66              .getConnection("jdbc:sqlite:C:\\Users\\spiro\\
              IdeaProjects\\e-coin\\db\\blockchain.db");
67     Statement blockchainStmt =
                  blockchainConnection.createStatement();
68     blockchainStmt.executeUpdate("CREATE TABLE IF NOT EXISTS
       BLOCKCHAIN ( " +
69                      " ID INTEGER NOT NULL UNIQUE, " +
70                      " PREVIOUS_HASH BLOB UNIQUE, " +
71                      " CURRENT_HASH BLOB UNIQUE, " +
72                      " LEDGER_ID INTEGER NOT NULL UNIQUE, " +
73                      " CREATED_ON  TEXT, " +
74                      " CREATED_BY  BLOB, " +
75                      " MINING_POINTS  TEXT, " +
76                      " LUCK  NUMERIC, " +
```

```
77                          " PRIMARY KEY( ID AUTOINCREMENT) " +
78                          ")"
79              );
```

Lines 65 and 66 will check and create a new `blockchain.db` file if it doesn't exist and establish a connection to it the same as we did on lines 38 and 39 previously for our `wallet.db`. Lines 67 to 79 will prepare and execute a statement that will check if the `BLOCKCHAIN` table exist in our `blockchain.db` and create one identical to the one shown in Figure 3-4.

On our next code snippet, we will be creating the functionality for our app to create the first block in our blockchain if it's not already present. It follows a similar logic as the one we used to check whether our `wallet.db` contained any data:

```
80      ResultSet resultSetBlockchain = blockchainStmt.execute
        Query(" SELECT * FROM BLOCKCHAIN ");
81      Transaction initBlockRewardTransaction = null;
82      if (!resultSetBlockchain.next()) {
83      Block firstBlock = new Block();
84      firstBlock.setMinedBy(WalletData.getInstance()
        .getWallet().getPublicKey().getEncoded());
85      firstBlock.setTimeStamp(LocalDateTime.now().toString());
86      //helper class.
87      Signature signing = Signature.getInstance("SHA256
        withDSA");
88      signing.initSign(WalletData.getInstance()
        .getWallet().getPrivateKey());
89      signing.update(firstBlock.toString().getBytes());
90      firstBlock.setCurrHash(signing.sign());
91      PreparedStatement pstmt = blockchainConnection
92          .prepareStatement("INSERT INTO BLOCKCHAIN
            (PREVIOUS_HASH,
            CURRENT_HASH , LEDGER_ID," +
```

```
93              " CREATED_ON, CREATED_BY,MINING_POINTS,LUCK ) " +
94              " VALUES (?,?,?,?,?,?,?) ");
95       pstmt.setBytes(1, firstBlock.getPrevHash());
96       pstmt.setBytes(2, firstBlock.getCurrHash());
97       pstmt.setInt(3, firstBlock.getLedgerId());
98       pstmt.setString(4, firstBlock.getTimeStamp());
99       pstmt.setBytes(5, WalletData.getInstance().getWallet()
         .getPublicKey().getEncoded());
100      pstmt.setInt(6, firstBlock.getMiningPoints());
101      pstmt.setDouble(7, firstBlock.getLuck());
102      pstmt.executeUpdate();
103      Signature transSignature = Signature
         .getInstance("SHA256withDSA");
104      initBlockRewardTransaction = new Transaction(WalletData
         .getInstance().getWallet(),WalletData.getInstance()
         .getWallet().getPublicKey()
         .getEncoded(),100,1,transSignature);
105    }
106    resultSetBlockchain.close();
107
```

Line 80 queries our BLOCKCHAIN table, and line 82 checks if there is blockchain present; if not, it executes lines 83–105. Line 83 uses our third block constructor. Line 84 retrieves our public key from the WalletData singleton class and sets us as the creators/miners of the initial block. Line 85 sets the timestamp. Lines 87 to 90 instantiate and use the Signature class from java.security to encrypt all of the data contained in the block by using the private key of the creator/miner of the block and set it as our current hash. This same process was observed in Figure 2-1 and explained in more detail there. Lines 91–102 export the data for our initial block from our app to our BLOCKCHAIN table. On lines 103 and 104 we prepare the initial block reward transaction for our block. We wait to transfer it to the TRANSACTIONS table since we still are not sure if it exists in the database. Let's look at the following code snippet where we handle the TRANSACTIONS table:

```
107
108             blockchainStmt.executeUpdate("CREATE
                TABLE IF NOT
                EXISTS TRANSACTIONS ( " +
109                     " ID INTEGER NOT NULL UNIQUE, " +
110                     " \"FROM\" BLOB, " +
111                     " \"TO\" BLOB, " +
112                     " LEDGER_ID INTEGER, " +
113                     " VALUE INTEGER, " +
114                     " SIGNATURE BLOB UNIQUE, " +
115                     " CREATED_ON TEXT, " +
116                     " PRIMARY KEY(ID AUTOINCREMENT) " +
117                     ")"
118             );
119             if (initBlockRewardTransaction != null) {
120               BlockchainData.getInstance()
                    .addTransaction(initBlockRewardTransaction,
                    true);
121               BlockchainData.getInstance()
                   .addTransactionState(initBlockReward
                   Transaction);
122             }
123             blockchainStmt.close();
124             blockchainConnection.close();
125         } catch (SQLException | NoSuchAlgorithmException |
            InvalidKeyException | SignatureException e) {
126             System.out.println("db failed: " +
                e.getMessage());
```

```
127         } catch (GeneralSecurityException e) {
128             e.printStackTrace();
129         }
130         BlockchainData.getInstance().loadBlockChain();
131     }
132}
```

On lines 108 to 118 we check if the TRANSACTIONS table exists and create it if it doesn't in much the same way as we did with our previous tables. Line 119 checks if we have initial reward transaction created, and if we do, lines 120 and 121 transfer it to the database and set our application state. Our last statement on line 130 shows our singleton class BlockData being loaded up with the data contained in our blockhain.db database. In our next chapter we will explain how this is achieved.

3.6 Summary

In this chapter, we covered the creation of two different databases that will support our application. We also created our init() method with functionality that allows easy portability and creation of wallets. Also, we made sure that our application is capable of creating the first block in our blockchain when no blockchain is present. This is a small recap of what concepts we covered so far:

- Creation of databases and table schemas using the database browser program
- Creation of our application's main class
- Creation of our start(Stage s) method
- Setting up the SQLite driver in Java and using it to create and query databases using Java and SQL
- Creating business logic for our app's init() method by using the SQLite driver and Java

CHAPTER 4

Building the UI

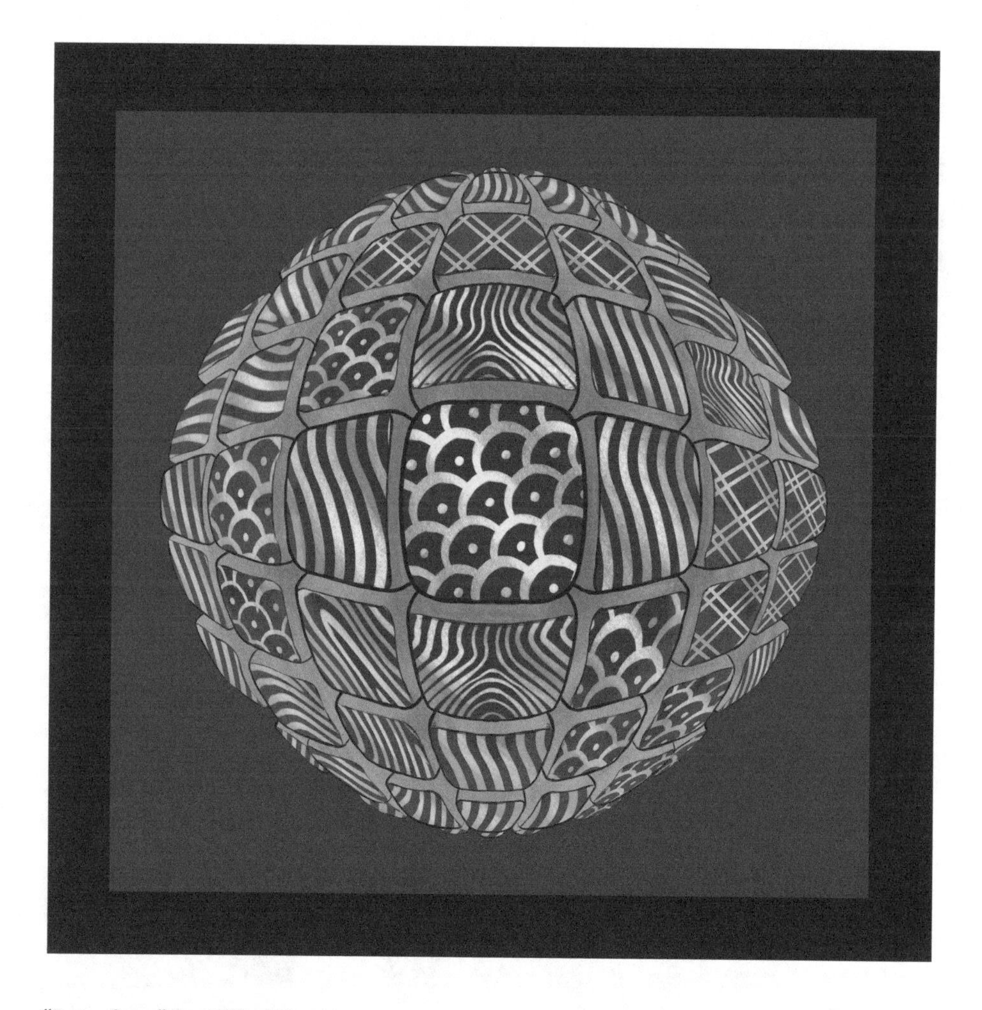

"Interface" by Filip Rizov

S. Buzharovski, *Introducing Blockchain with Java*,
https://doi.org/10.1007/978-1-4842-7927-4_4

This chapter will cover how to create our UI. Using the UI we will be able to check our coin balance, display our public address so that we can share it with others, look at recent transactions, and send coins to others. For this purpose, we will use Scene Builder, a GUI tool that will help us create our front end. For our controller classes, we will be using Java and JavaFX. Finally, we will explain how to create our separate UI thread that will listen for our input.

4.1 Scene Builder Quick Setup

Download Scene Builder by visiting `https://gluonhq.com/products/scene-builder/`. The page will display different options, as shown in Figure 4-1.

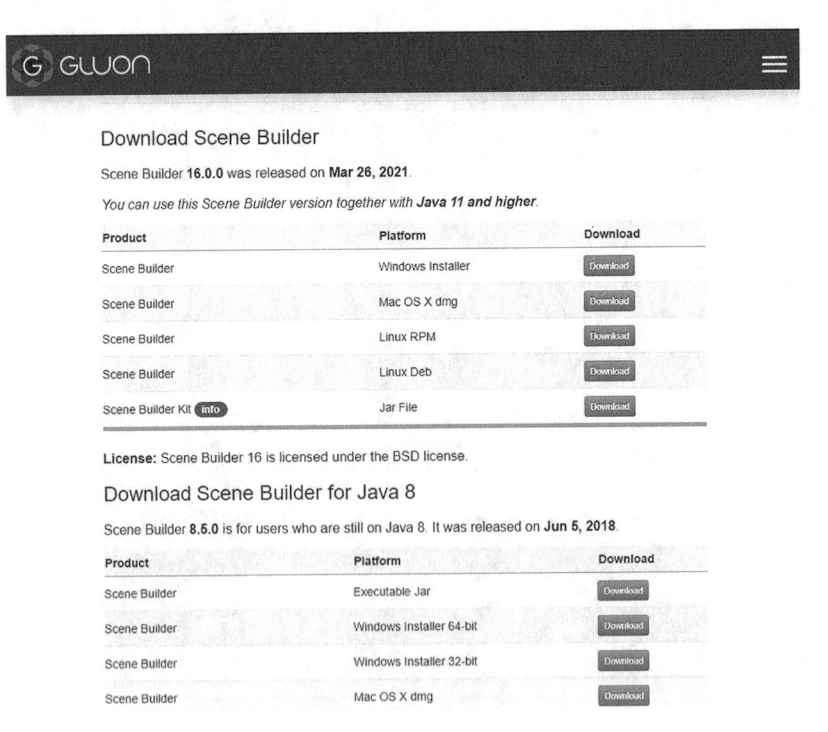

Figure 4-1. *The Scene Builder download page*

Simply choose the appropriate download depending on your OS. Install the app following the provided instructions and you are good to go.

4.2 Creating Your Views

In the next sections we will explain how to create our views by using Scene Builder. It's recommended that you create a `View` folder within the folder structure shown in Figure 4-2. This is where we will create and keep our view classes.

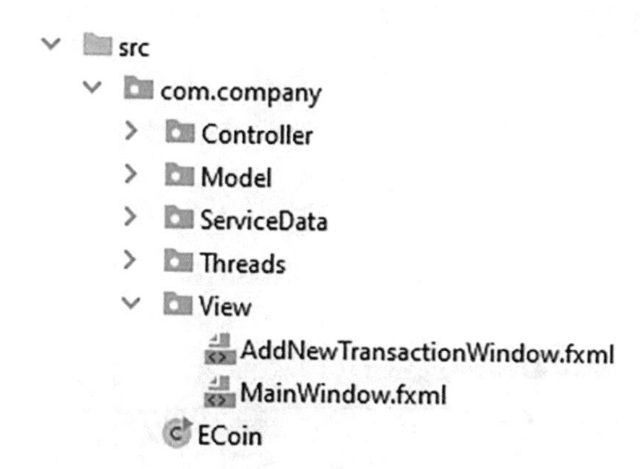

Figure 4-2. *Creating the folder structure*

4.2.1 MainWindow.fxml

Let's create our `MainWindow.fxml` file. First start Scene Builder and choose an empty scene, as shown in Figure 4-3.

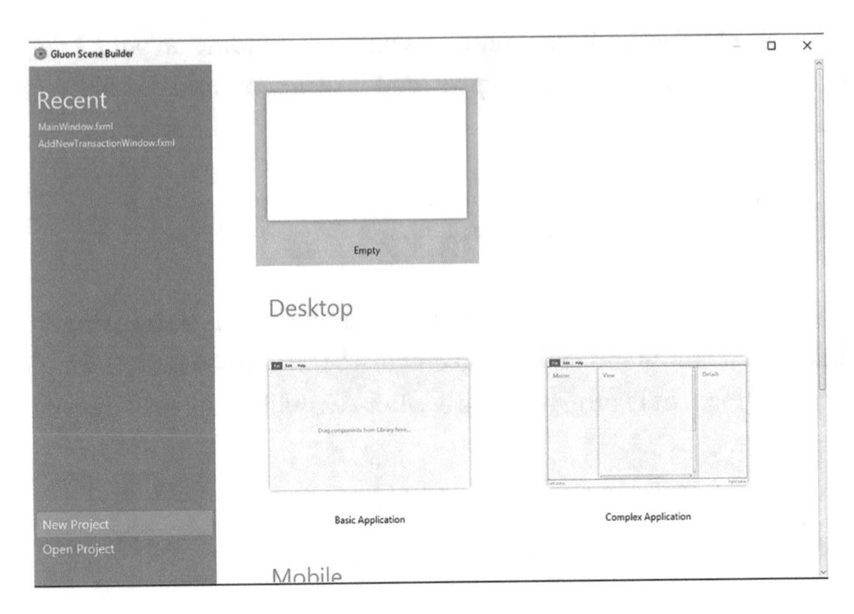

Figure 4-3. *Choosing an empty scene*

Once you do this, your next screen should look like Figure 4-4.

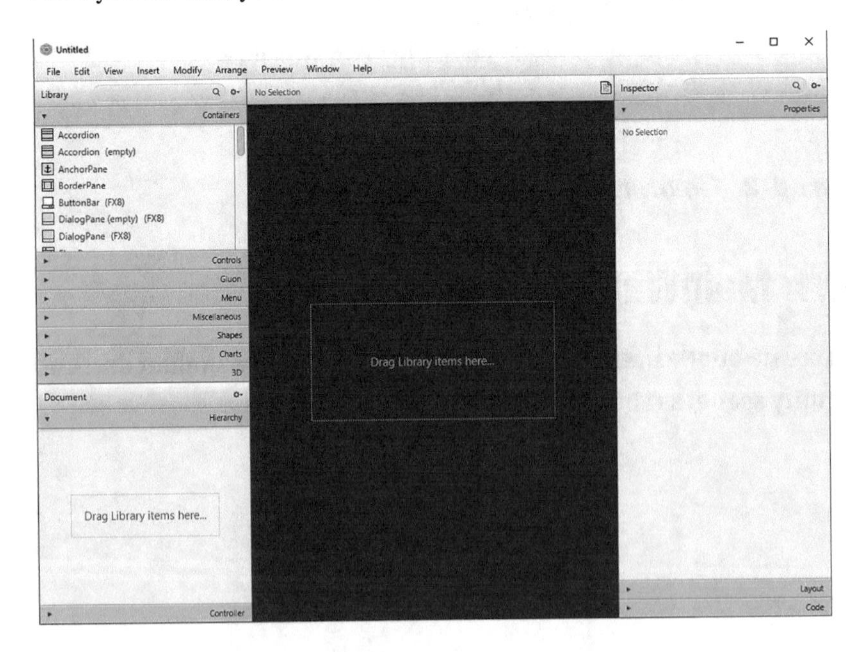

Figure 4-4. *The empty screen*

This means that we are ready to start creating our `MainWindow.fxml` file, but first let's explain some of the elements we are seeing in Figure 4-4. In the top-left side of the screen, we can see the premade visual elements that are used to create views by dragging and dropping them in the middle of the screen or onto the Hierarchy tab. You can also notice that different types of elements are grouped under different tabs such as Containers, Controls, etc. In the bottom left of the screen, we can see the Hierarchy tab; here we can observe the element structure of our scene. Below the Hierarchy tab we have the Controller tab, where we can see information regarding the location of our controller for this view and the fields associated with our view elements. In the middle we can see a preview of how our view will appear. On the right side of the screen we can see three tabs called Properties, Layout, and Code, which is where we can adjust and customize each element's attributes. Before we start adding visual elements to our scene, let's first save this file in our `View` folder and name it `MainWindow.fxml`, as shown in Figure 4-5.

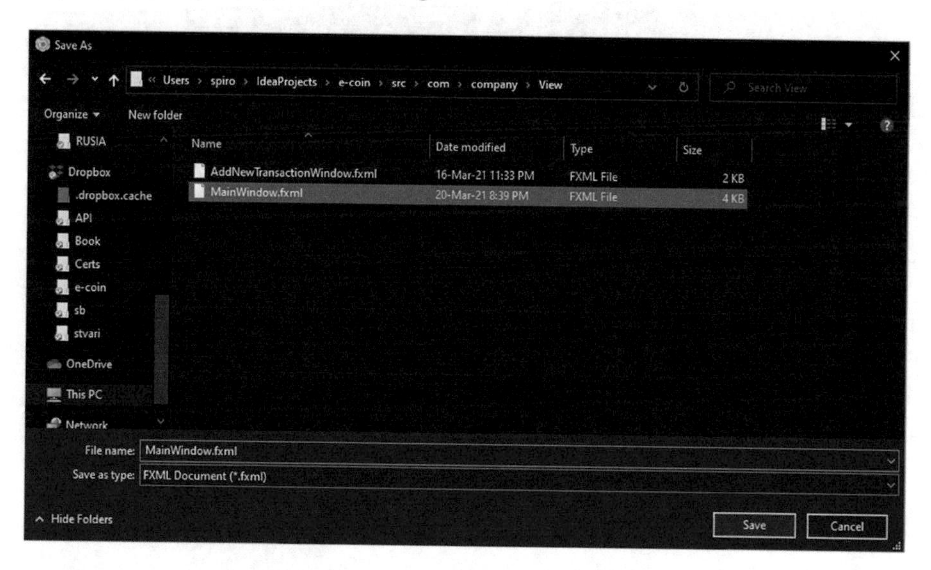

Figure 4-5. *Saving the file*

Let's start creating our front-end scene by dragging a BorderPane element from the Containers tab into the middle of the screen. Your screen should look like Figure 4-6.

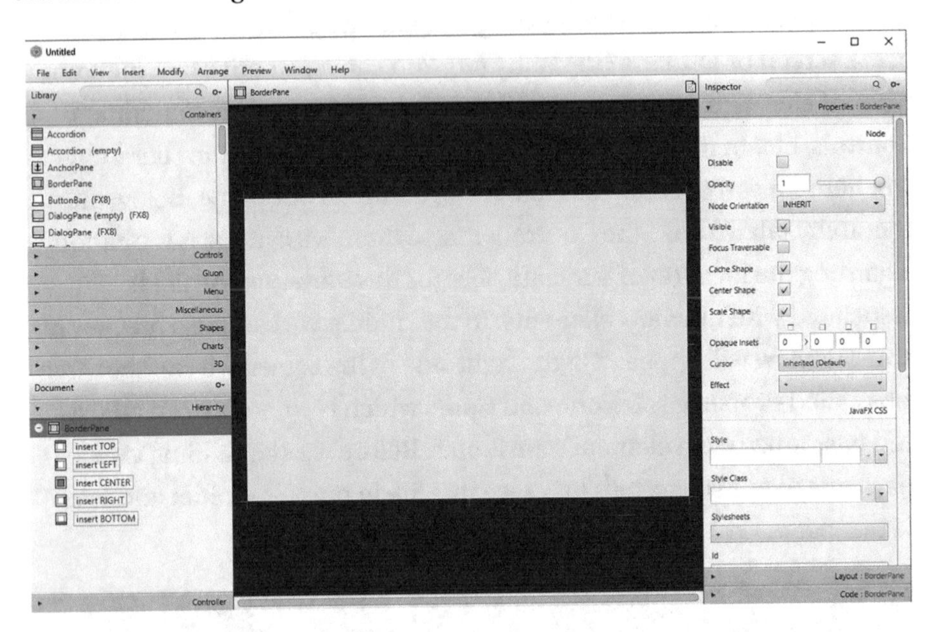

Figure 4-6. *Adding a BorderPane*

Notice the BorderPane element in the Hierarchy tab together with its subelements. Next let's drag a MenuBar from the Controls tab and drop it into the TOP subelement of our BorderPane, as shown in Figure 4-7.

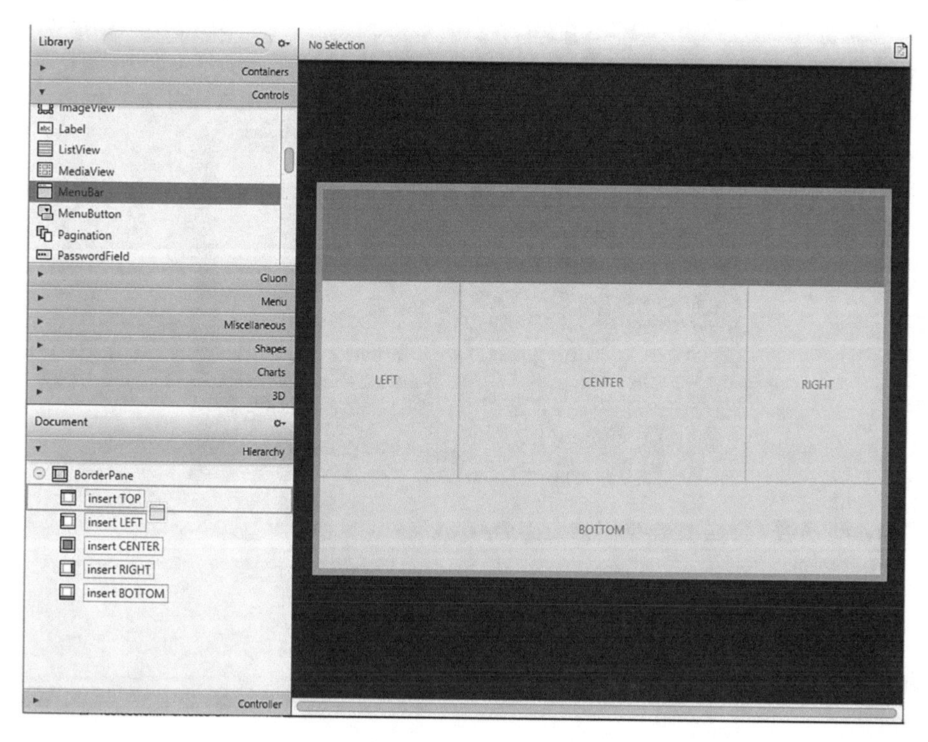

Figure 4-7. *Adding a MenuBar*

If you click the + next to the MenuBar element, you will notice that it comes with three menu subelements named File, Edit, and Help. Since we are only going to use the File subelement, let's delete the Edit and Help subelements by right-clicking them and selecting Delete from the drop-down menu, as shown in Figure 4-8.

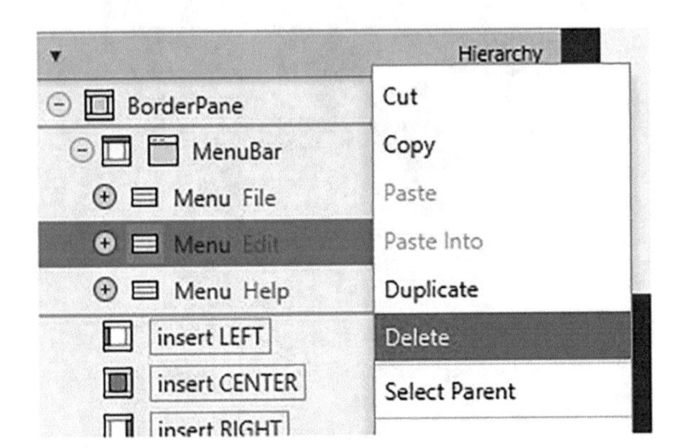

***Figure 4-8.** Deleting some submenus*

Now let's expand the File submenu. Here you will notice that we have another nested element called MenuItem named Close. Let's add another MenuItem element and name it Make Transaction. To do this, first let's open the Menu tab and drag another MenuItem element and drop it right above the Close MenuItem, as shown on Figure 4-9.

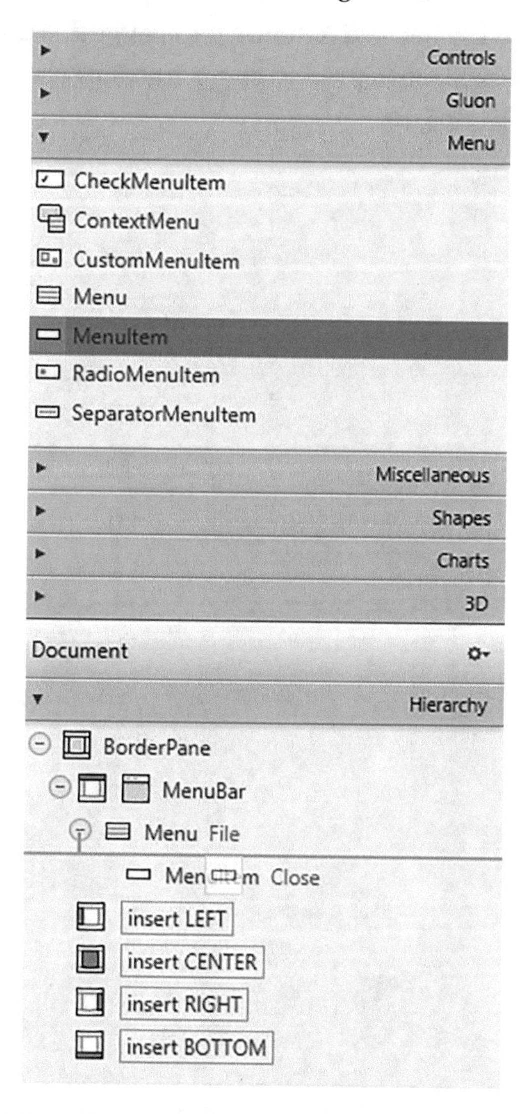

Figure 4-9. *Adding elements*

As you are dragging the MenuItem element, notice the orange line that will help you visualize where the item will be placed once you drop it. You will notice that this MenuItem gets named by default as Unspecified Action. Let's select this element by clicking it in the Hierarchy tab and then expand the Properties tab. You will notice a property called *text* that has a text value named Unspecified Action. Let's change this value to **Make Transaction**, which effectively renames our element. The final result should look like Figure 4-10.

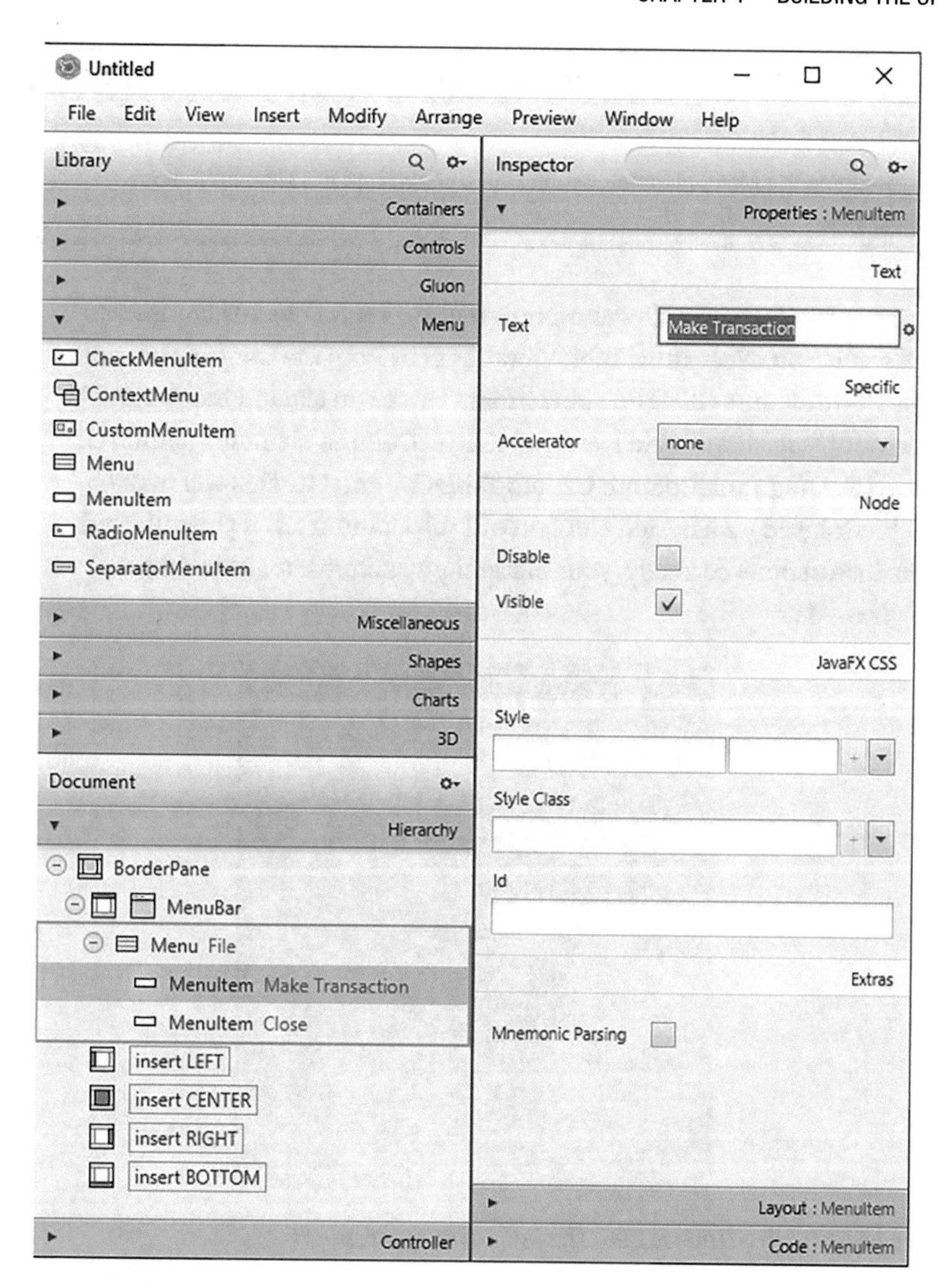

Figure 4-10. *Renaming the text element*

EXERCISE 4-1

Rename the Menu element named File to **Menu** and the MenuItem Close to **Exit**.

We are finished with our MenuBar and its subelements for now, so let's move on. Next add a TableView element from the Controls tab onto the BorderPane's CENTER subelement. Once you expand the TableView element, you should find two nested TableColumn elements named C1 and C2. Drag TableColumn C2 into TableColumn C1. This will make TableColumn C2 a nested element of TableColumn C1. If you followed the instructions correctly, your hierarchy structure should look like Figure 4-11.

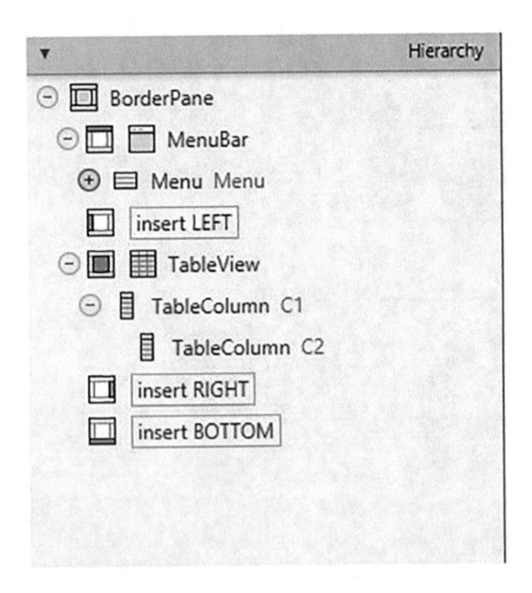

Figure 4-11. *Two nested TableColumn elements*

Let's add four more TableColumn elements from the Controls tab as nested elements of TableColumn C1. In this table view that we are creating we would like to be able to display our current block transactions with the associated details, so we should rename our table columns accordingly such as C1 to **Current Block Transactions** and then all the nested table columns in order like this: **From, To, Value, Signature**, and **Created On**. If you have done things correctly, your screen should look like Figure 4-12.

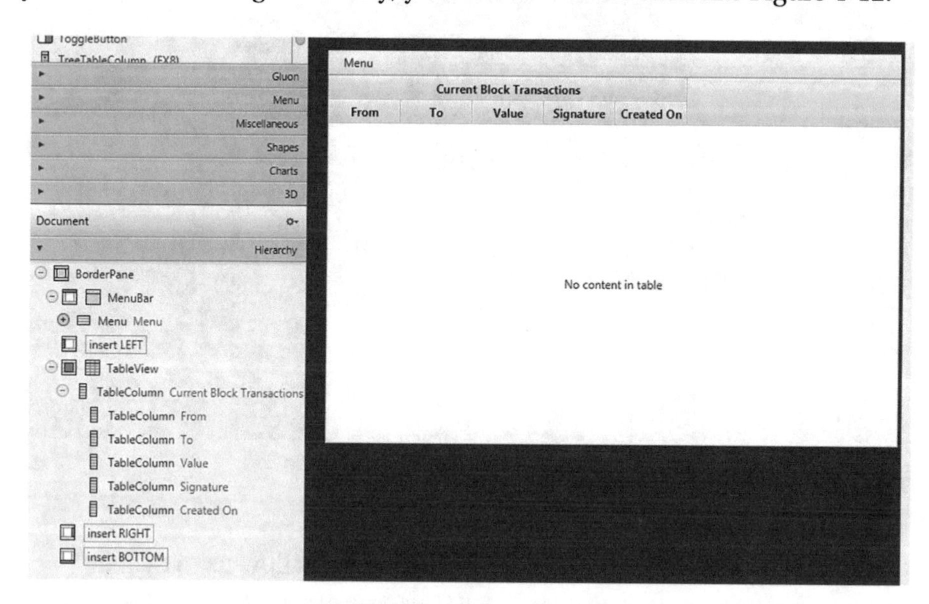

Figure 4-12. *The finished table columns*

You have most likely noticed that the width of our table columns doesn't cover the whole area of our screen. To fix the width of our table columns, select the TableView element, go into its Properties tab to find the Column Resize Policy attribute, and select constrained-resize, as shown in Figure 4-13.

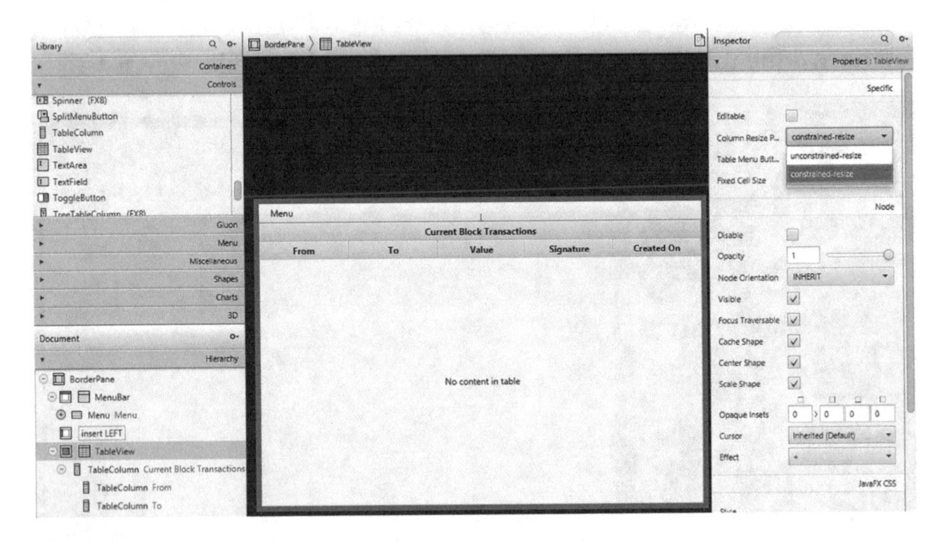

Figure 4-13. *Resizing the table columns*

Our next task is to add some elements that will allow us to display our coins balance, our public key/wallet address, and a button that will refresh our UI and retrieve the latest information regarding transactions and our balance. We will do this by dragging another BorderPane from the Containers tab inside the BOTTOM section of our existing BorderPane. This new BorderPane will come with its own existing TOP, LEFT, CENTER, RIGHT, and BOTTOM sections. In other words, this new BorderPane subdivides the bottom section of the first BorderPane into five new sections, as shown in Figure 4-14.

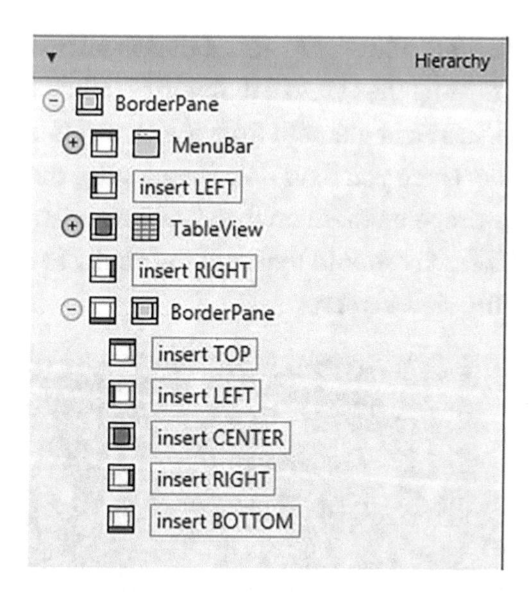

Figure 4-14. *New BorderPane*

This will allow us to position the elements, we mentioned earlier, in their own separate sections, which helps organize our hierarchy structure. Now let's insert an AnchorPane from the Containers tab into the LEFT, CENTER, and RIGHT sections of our new BorderPane, as shown in Figure 4-15.

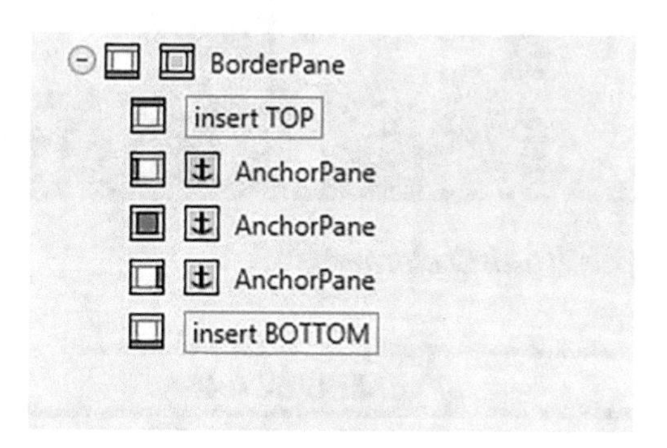

Figure 4-15. *Inserting an AnchorPane*

The AnchorPane will allow us to adjust the visual position of our elements just by dragging them into a different position. Now let's drag and drop a Label and a TextField element from the Controls tabs into our LEFT section AnchorPane. Once you have done that, notice that you can easily reposition them by dragging them on the view screen itself. Figure 4-16 shows how your hierarchy should look and the ability to drag and align your elements on the view screen.

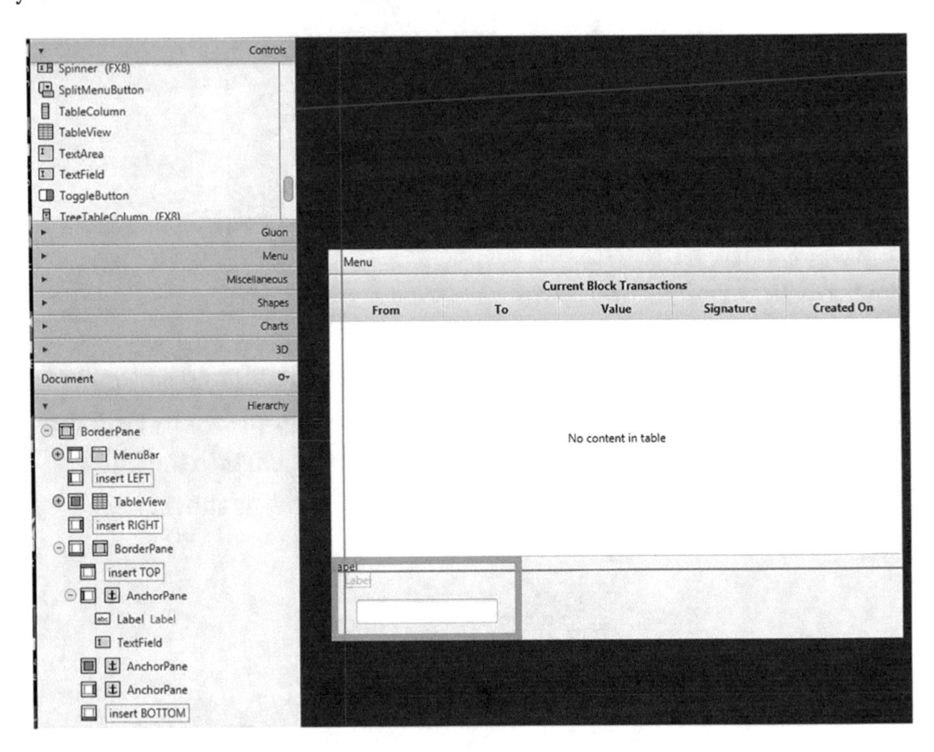

Figure 4-16. Repositioning elements

EXERCISE 4-2

Rename the Label element named Label to **Your Balance:** and reposition it and the TextField element so they look better visually.

Next let's drop a Label and TextArea element from the Controls tab into our CENTER section AnchorPane and a Button from the same tab into our RIGHT section AnchorPane. Your hierarchy structure should look like Figure 4-17.

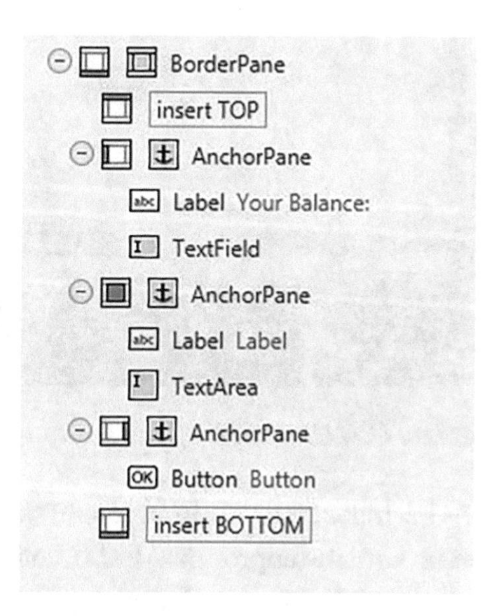

Figure 4-17. *Adding a Label and TextArea to CENTER*

EXERCISE 4-3

Rename the Label element named Label to **Your Address / Public Key:**, rename the Button from Button to **Refresh**, and then reposition them to look better visually.

In Figure 4-18 you can see the complete UX/UI design of our scene with its expanded structure hierarchy. This is a good figure to review and check if you have missed something in your own scene.

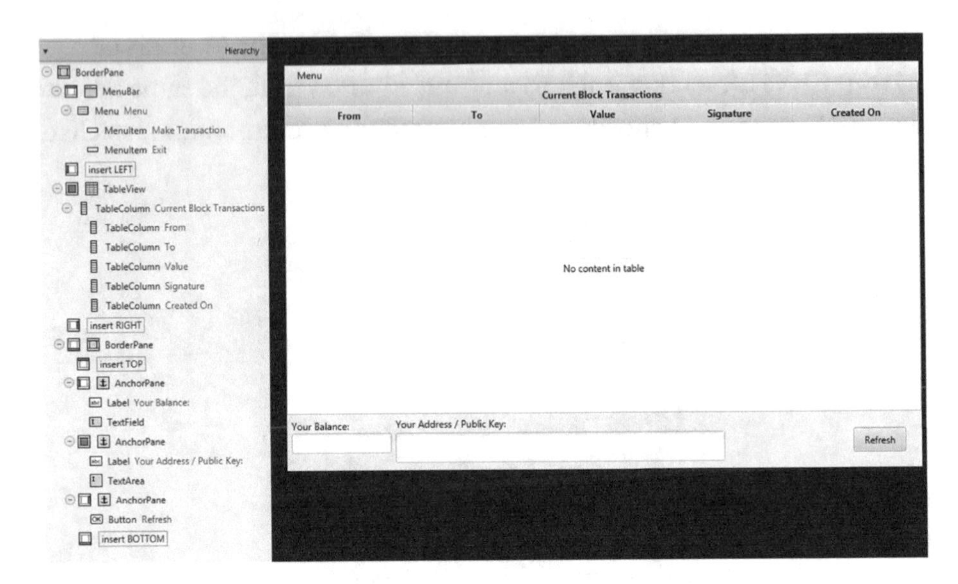

***Figure 4-18.** Complete UX/UI design of our scene*

If you open the `MainWindow.fxml` file from IntelliJ now, you will notice that it has been filled up with the appropriate FXML code by Scene Builder automatically. Keep in mind that you need to save your changes in Scene Builder before the code in the FXML file gets generated. Also make sure to save the latest changes in Scene Builder and exit if you intend to change the FXML file manually; otherwise, you might desynchronize the work from Scene Builder and your local file and lose some of the changes.

Until this point we have worked only on the visual design of our scene. We have all our elements positioned the way we want them, but what we are missing now are references to our back-end methods and fields so that we can use them. First let's add the file path of our future controller class for this scene. This will create a link in the application between our view and its controller. In other words, the application will try to find and run/display any methods or fields that we will reference in the view from its corresponding controller class. To add the file path of our controller class, open the Controller tab in the bottom-left side of your screen and enter it in the Controller class text field, as shown in Figure 4-19.

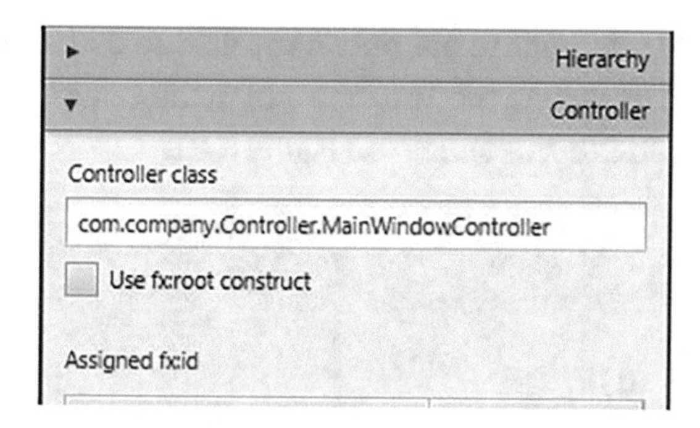

Figure 4-19. *Adding the file path of our controller class*

Now let's add a reference to the method that our refresh button should call once we click it. To do that, select our refresh button, expand its Code tab from the bottom-right side of the screen, and enter the method name in the On Action text field, which will be **refresh**, as shown in Figure 4-20.

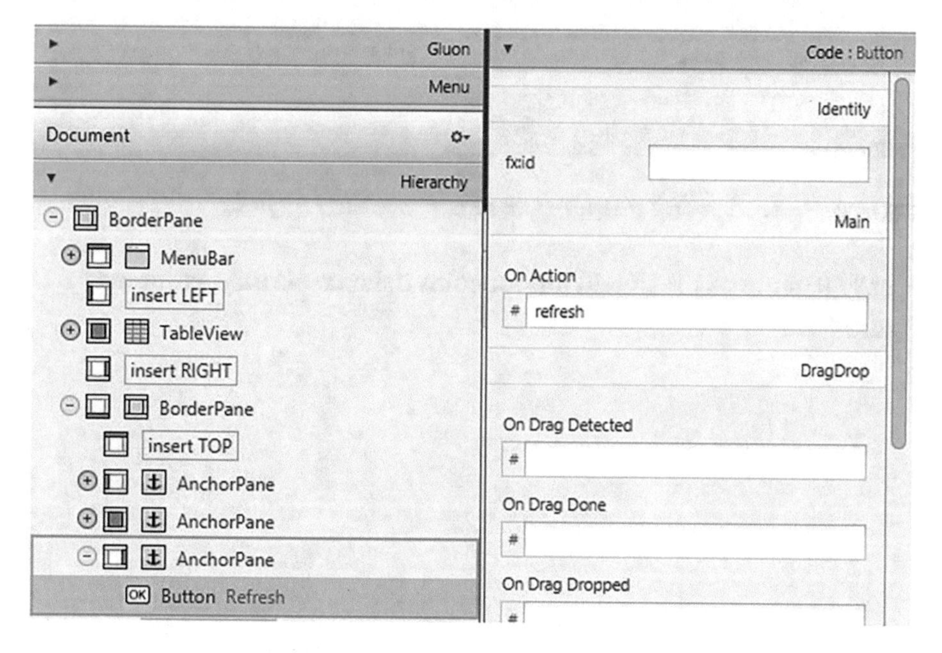

Figure 4-20. *Adding a refresh button*

Next let's add reference to our public key field so that we can display it in our TextArea. Let's select the TextArea and in the Code tab find the fx:id field; name it **publicKey**, as shown on Figure 4-21.

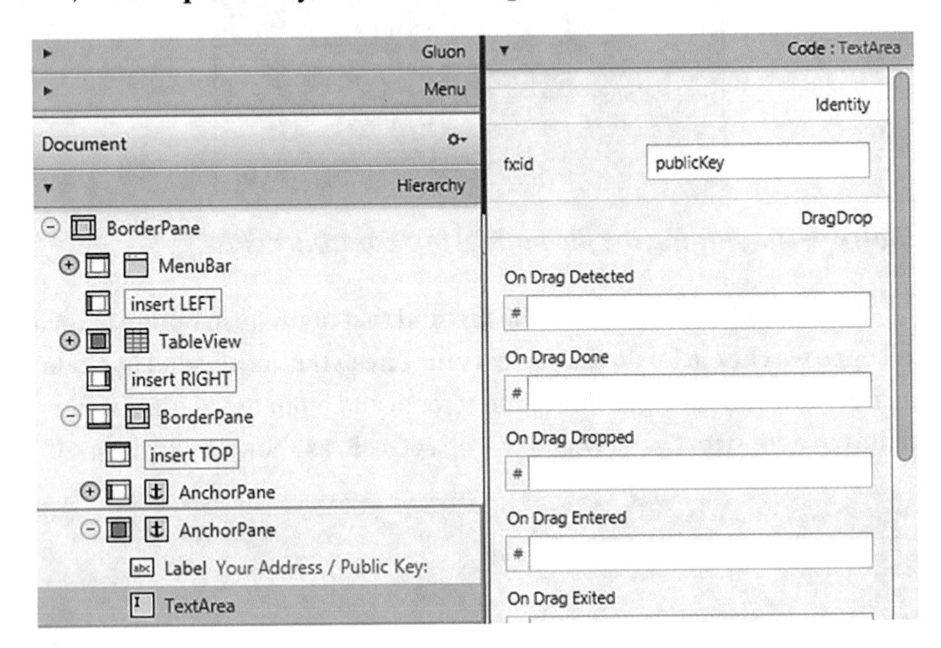

***Figure 4-21.** Adding a reference to our public key field*

We'll name our TextField for our coins balance **eCoins**, as shown in Figure 4-22.

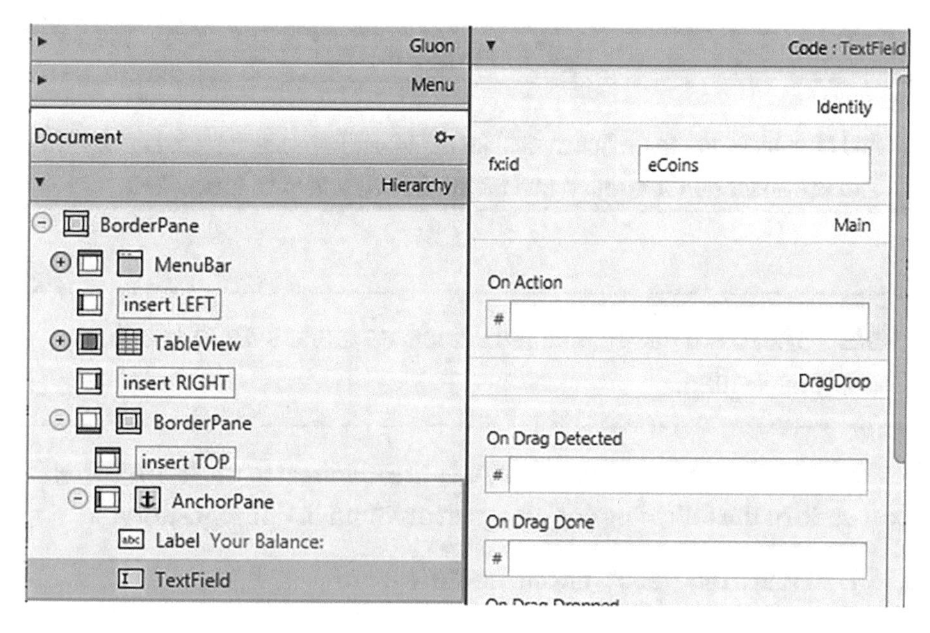

Figure 4-22. *Naming our coins balance*

Now that we've shown you how to add controller references, you should be able to finish adding the rest on your own.

EXERCISE 4-4

Add references to the fx:id field for our first BorderPane as **borderPane**, for our TableView as **tableview**, for our From TableColum as **from**, for our To TableColumn as **to**, for our Value TableColumn as **value**, for our Signature TableColumn as **signature**, for our Created On TableColumn as **timestamp**.

Note These are case-sensitive values, so make sure to add them exactly as written.

EXERCISE 4-5

Add references to the On Action field for our Make Transaction MenuItem as **toNewTransactionController**, and for the Exit MenuItem as **handleExit**.

Note These are case-sensitive values, so make sure to add them exactly as written.

Double-check to see if your changes are identical to the `MainWindow.fxml` code in the following code snippet or found in our repository:

```
1  <?xml version="1.0" encoding="UTF-8"?>
2
3  <?import javafx.scene.control.Button?>
4  <?import javafx.scene.control.Label?>
5  <?import javafx.scene.control.Menu?>
6  <?import javafx.scene.control.MenuBar?>
7  <?import javafx.scene.control.MenuItem?>
8  <?import javafx.scene.control.TableColumn?>
9  <?import javafx.scene.control.TableView?>
10 <?import javafx.scene.control.TextArea?>
11 <?import javafx.scene.control.TextField?>
12 <?import javafx.scene.layout.AnchorPane?>
13 <?import javafx.scene.layout.BorderPane?>
14
15 <BorderPane fx:id="borderPane" maxHeight="-Infinity"
   maxWidth=" -Infinity" minHeight="-Infinity" minWidth="-
   Infinity"
```

```
16     prefHeight="500.0" prefWidth="800.0"
       xmlns="http://javafx.com/javafx/15.0.1"
       xmlns:fx="http://javafx.com/fxml/1"
17     fx:controller="com.company.Controller.MainWindow
       Controller">
18     <top>
19         <MenuBar prefHeight="25.0" prefWidth="800.0"
              BorderPane.alignment="CENTER">
20             <menus>
21                 <Menu mnemonicParsing="false" text="Menu">
22                     <items>
23                         <MenuItem mnemonicParsing="false"
                          onAction="#toNewTransactionController"
                          text="Make Transaction" />
24                         <MenuItem mnemonicParsing="false"
                           onAction="#handleExit" text="Exit" />
25                     </items>
26                 </Menu>
27             </menus>
28         </MenuBar>
29     </top>
30     <center>
31         <TableView fx:id="tableview" prefHeight="406.0"
              prefWidth="800.0" BorderPane.alignment="CENTER">
32             <columns>
33             <TableColumn prefWidth="75.0" text="Current Block
                Transactions">
34                 <columns>
35                     <TableColumn fx:id="from" prefWidth="160"
                       text="From" />
```

```
36                      <TableColumn fx:id="to" prefWidth="160"
                        text="To" />
37                      <TableColumn fx:id="value" prefWidth="160"
                        text="Value" />
38                      <TableColumn fx:id="signature"
                        prefWidth="160" text="Signature" />
39                      <TableColumn fx:id="timestamp"
                        prefWidth="160" text="Created On" />
40                   </columns>
41                </TableColumn>
42                </columns>
43             <columnResizePolicy>
44                <TableView fx:constant="CONSTRAINED_RESIZE_
                  POLICY" />
45             </columnResizePolicy>
46          </TableView>
47      </center>
48     <bottom>
49        <BorderPane prefHeight="69.0" prefWidth="800.0">
50           <center>
51              <AnchorPane prefHeight="83.0" prefWidth="269.0"
                   BorderPane.alignment="CENTER">
52                 <children>
53                    <Label layoutY="4.0" prefHeight="17.0"
                        prefWidth="149.0" text="Your Address /
                        Public Key:" />
54                    <TextArea fx:id="publicKey"
                      editable="false"
                        layoutY="23.0" prefHeight="36.0"
                        prefWidth="416.0" />
55                 </children>
```

```
56              </AnchorPane>
57          </center>
58          <left>
59              <AnchorPane prefHeight="56.0" prefWidth="136.0"
                    BorderPane.alignment="CENTER">
60                  <children>
61                      <Label layoutX="6.0" layoutY="6.0"
                         prefHeight="17.0" prefWidth="84.0"
                         text="Your Balance:" />
62                      <TextField fx:id="eCoins" editable="false"
                         layoutX="6.0" layoutY="23.0"
                         prefHeight="25.0" prefWidth="125.0" />
63                  </children>
64              </AnchorPane>
65          </left>
66          <right>
67              <AnchorPane prefHeight="200.0" prefWidth="200.0"
                    BorderPane.alignment="CENTER">
68                  <children>
69                   <Button layoutX="113.0" layoutY="20.0"
                        mnemonicParsing="false"
                        nodeOrientation="LEFT_TO_RIGHT"
                        onAction="#refresh" prefHeight="30.0"
70                          prefWidth="67.0" text="Refresh"
                            textAlignment="CENTER" />
71                  </children>
72              </AnchorPane>
73          </right>
74      </BorderPane>
75   </bottom>
76 </BorderPane>
77
```

With the exercises complete, we now have our main window scene completely finished. If you open the file in IntelliJ, it will show you some errors since the references we added don't exist yet, but we are about to fix that in our following sections.

4.2.2 AddNewTransactionWindow.fxml

Since by now we have explained everything you need to know to create your own view in Scene Builder, it's time for you to create the scene from this section by performing the following exercises.

EXERCISE 4-6

Open a new file in Scene Builder and save it in the same folder structure as our previous scene. Name the file `AddNewTransactionWindow.fxml`.

EXERCISE 4-7

Create your scene with the hierarchy structure and appearance shown in Figure 4-23. Add the controller class path as `com.company.Controller.AddNewTransactionController`.

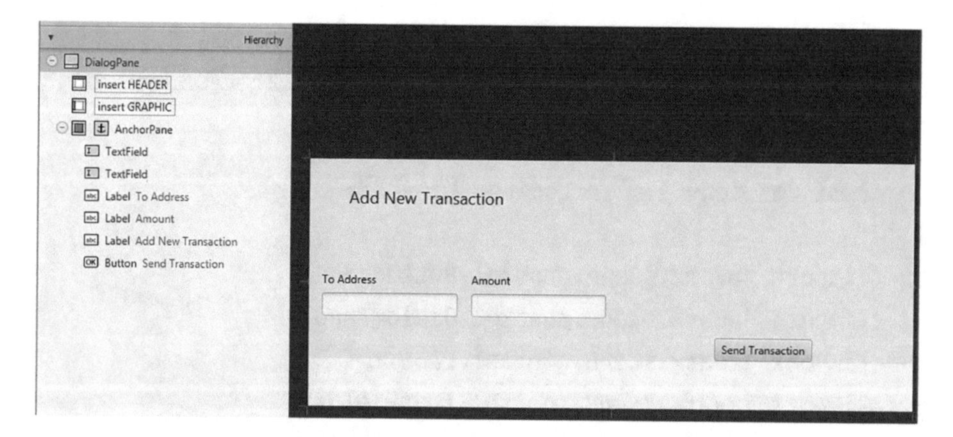

Figure 4-23. *Adding the controller class*

EXERCISE 4-8

Add the controller class path as `com.company.Controller.AddNewTransactionController`.

EXERCISE 4-9

Add references to the fx:id field for our To Address TextField as **toAddress** and for our Amount TextField as **value**.

EXERCISE 4-10

Add references to the On Action field for our Send Transaction Button as **createNewTransaction**.

Double-check to see if your changes are identical to the AddNewTransactionWindow.fxml code in the following code snippet or found in our repository:

```
1  <?xml version="1.0" encoding="UTF-8"?>
2
3  <?import javafx.scene.control.Button?>
4  <?import javafx.scene.control.DialogPane?>
5  <?import javafx.scene.control.Label?>
6  <?import javafx.scene.control.TextField?>
7  <?import javafx.scene.layout.AnchorPane?>
8  <?import javafx.scene.text.Font?>
9
10 <DialogPane prefHeight="266.0" prefWidth="667.0"
   xmlns="http://javafx.com/javafx/15.0.1" xmlns:fx="http://
   javafx.com/fxml/1" fx:controller="com.company.Controller.
   AddNewTransactionController">
11    <content>
12        <AnchorPane minHeight="0.0" minWidth="0.0"
             prefHeight="250.0" prefWidth="657.0">
13            <children>
14                <TextField fx:id="toAddress"
                   layoutX="14.0" layoutY="144.0" />
15                <TextField fx:id="value"
                   layoutX="178.0" layoutY="144.0" />
16                <Label layoutX="14.0" layoutY="121.0"
                   text="To Address" />
17                <Label layoutX="178.0" layoutY="121.0"
                   text="Amount" />
18                <Label layoutX="43.0" layoutY="28.0"
                   text="Add New Transaction">
```

```
19                              <font>
20                                  <Font size="18.0" />
21                              </font>
22                          </Label>
23                          <Button layoutX="447.0" layoutY="189.0"
                             mnemonicParsing="false"
                             onAction="#createNewTransaction"
                             text="Send Transaction" />
24                      </children>
25                  </AnchorPane>
26              </content>
27  </DialogPane>
28
```

4.3 Creating Your View Controllers

Once we have our view classes finished, it's time for us to create their controllers. We will start by adding a folder named `Controller` in the same folder path as our `View` folder, as shown in Figure 4-24.

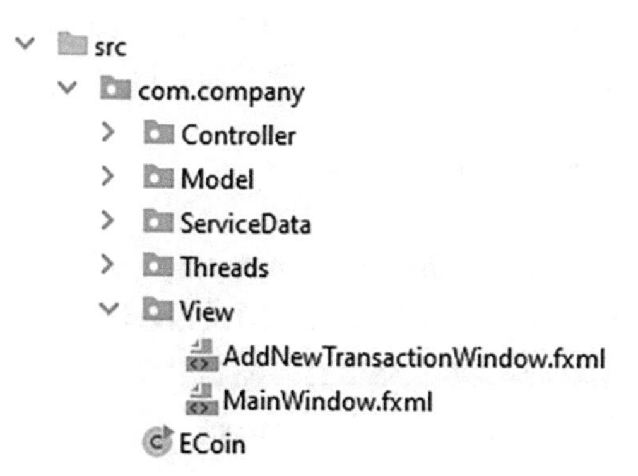

Figure 4-24. *Adding a folder*

Before we move on to explain the code in the controllers, let's quickly download and install an encoder library called Base64, which will help us convert our public keys that are stored as byte arrays into strings, and vice versa. This is important because the standard Java encoder while converting byte arrays to strings will change the contents of the byte arrays, which will make them invalid as a public key. To install our Base64 library, let's visit `http://migbase64.sourceforge.net/` and download it. Once we download it, we will need to unzip it and place in it the `libs` folder next to our SQLite driver, as shown in Figure 4-25.

e-coin C:\Users\spiro\IdeaProjects\e-coin
.idea
db
libs
Base64.java
sqlite-jdbc-3.34.0.jar

Figure 4-25. *Installing the encoder library called Base64*

4.3.1 MainWindowController

Let's observe our imports for the `MainWindowController` class in the following code snippet:

```
1  package com.company.Controller;
2
3  import com.company.Model.Transaction;
4  import com.company.ServiceData.BlockchainData;
5  import com.company.ServiceData.WalletData;
6  import javafx.application.Platform;
7  import javafx.fxml.FXML;
8  import javafx.fxml.FXMLLoader;
9  import javafx.scene.control.*;
```

```
10 import javafx.scene.control.cell.PropertyValueFactory;
11 import javafx.scene.layout.BorderPane;
12
13 import java.io.IOException;
14 import java.util.Base64;
15 import java.util.Optional;
16
```

Next let's move on to the class fields as shown in the following snippet and explain them:

```
17 public class MainWindowController {
18     //this is read-only UI table
19     @FXML
20     public TableView<Transaction> tableview = new
       TableView<>();
21     @FXML
22     private TableColumn<Transaction, String> from;
23     @FXML
24     private TableColumn<Transaction, String> to;
25     @FXML
26     private TableColumn<Transaction, Integer> value;
27     @FXML
28     private TableColumn<Transaction, String> timestamp;
29     @FXML
30     private TableColumn<Transaction, String> signature;
31     @FXML
32     private BorderPane borderPane;
33     @FXML
34     private TextField eCoins;
35     @FXML
36     private TextArea publicKey;
37
```

You will recall how in the "MainWindow.fxml" section we added fx:id references for the fields in our controller class to some of our elements. Now it's time to create those fields. All the classes for these fields come from the javafx package, which is included in your Java SDK. We will need to annotate each element with the @FXML tag and name each field with the same name as our fx:id reference. If done properly, an icon next to the line number will appear, and if clicked, it will take you to the exact place in your FXML file where the field is referenced. Also make sure that the classes for our fields correspond to the types of elements we picked in our FXML file.

Now let's move on to our following code snippet where we will talk about our initialize() method for the controller:

```
38     public void initialize() {
39         Base64.Encoder encoder = Base64.getEncoder();
40         from.setCellValueFactory(
41                 new PropertyValueFactory<>("fromFX"));
42         to.setCellValueFactory(
43                 new PropertyValueFactory<>("toFX"));
44         value.setCellValueFactory(
45                 new PropertyValueFactory<>("value"));
46         signature.setCellValueFactory(
47                 new PropertyValueFactory<>("signatureFX"));
48         timestamp.setCellValueFactory(
49                 new PropertyValueFactory<>("timestamp"));
50         eCoins.setText(BlockchainData.getInstance()
                   .getWalletBallanceFX());
51         publicKey.setText(encoder.encodeToString(
               WalletData.getInstance().getWallet()
               .getPublicKey().getEncoded()));
```

```
52          tableview.setItems(BlockchainData
                .getInstance().getTransactionLedgerFX());
53          tableview.getSelectionModel().select(0);
54      }
55
```

On line 39 we initialize our Base64 encoder. On lines 40–49 we are creating cell value factories for our table columns. In other words, we reference the values from the fields of the class that our table view contains to be displayed in the appropriate columns. On line 50, we set the coins balance to be displayed. Here you will notice that we are using methods from our service layer to achieve this, which we will explain in detail in our next chapter. Line 51 uses the Base64 encoder to encode our public key, which we retrieve using our service layer classes, as a byte array and change it into a string to display it. On line 52 we retrieve the transactions we want to display by using the service layer method `BlockchainData.getInstance().getTransactionLedgerFX()` and then set them in our tableview to get displayed. Lastly, line 53 selects our first transaction by default.

Let's look at our final code snippet and explain the remaining methods:

```
56      @FXML
57      public void toNewTransactionController() {
58          Dialog<ButtonType> newTransactionController =
                new Dialog<>();
59          newTransactionController.initOwner(borderPane
              .getScene().getWindow());
60          FXMLLoader fxmlLoader = new FXMLLoader();
61          fxmlLoader.setLocation(getClass().getResource(
                "../View/AddNewTransactionWindow.fxml"));
```

```
62          try {
63              newTransactionController.getDialogPane()
                        .setContent(fxmlLoader.load());
64          } catch (IOException e) {
65              System.out.println("Cant load dialog");
66              e.printStackTrace();
67              return;
68          }
69          newTransactionController.getDialogPane()
                .getButtonTypes().add(ButtonType.FINISH);
70          Optional<ButtonType> result =
                              newTransactionController.showAndWait();
71          if (result.isPresent() ) {
72              tableview.setItems(BlockchainData.getInstance()
                   .getTransactionLedgerFX());
73              eCoins.setText(BlockchainData.getInstance()
                    .getWalletBallanceFX());
74          }
75      }
76
77      @FXML
78      public void refresh() {
79          tableview.setItems(BlockchainData.getInstance()
              .getTransactionLedgerFX());
80          tableview.getSelectionModel().select(0);
81          eCoins.setText(BlockchainData.getInstance()
              .getWalletBallanceFX());
82      }
83
84      @FXML
85      public void handleExit() {
```

```
86          BlockchainData.getInstance().setExit(true);
87          Platform.exit();
88      }
89 }
90
```

You will notice that, just like our fields, all of our methods are methods we referenced in our associated FXML file, which means we need to annotate them with the @FXML tag also.

Important! It's a great practice to keep the controller classes populated only with fields and methods that are used by the associated view. Any other computations or methods that might be required should be called from and handled by your service layer.

Let's start with our first method, `toNewTransactionController()`, on line 57. If you recall, we associated this method with our MenuItem named Make Transaction on the On Action field. This means that once we click the menu item, this method will run. What we want from this method is to initiate a new dialog and display the contents of our `AddNewTransactionController.fxml` file in it. Lines 58–68 achieve this. Line 69 will create a FINISH button, and line 70 will create a listener where it waits until it's clicked. Lines 71–74 refresh our transactions list and coins balance once the FINISH button is clicked.

On lines 78–83 we have our `refresh()` method, which is referenced in our refresh button. In other words, once our refresh button is clicked, it activates the refresh method, which uses our service layer to refresh our transaction and balance values.

Lastly our `handleExit()` method on line 87 sets a Boolean that will trigger all the parallel threads to exit their loops and finish, and line 88 tells our UI thread to finish.

4.3.2 AddNewTransactionController

Let's look at our second controller's code in AddNewTransactionController.fxml, as shown in the following snippet:

```
1  package com.company.Controller;
2
3  import com.company.Model.Transaction;
4  import com.company.ServiceData.BlockchainData;
5  import com.company.ServiceData.WalletData;
6  import javafx.fxml.FXML;
7  import javafx.scene.control.TextField;
8
9  import java.security.GeneralSecurityException;
10 import java.security.Signature;
11 import java.util.Base64;
12
13 public class AddNewTransactionController {
14
15     @FXML
16     private TextField toAddress;
17     @FXML
18     private TextField value;
19
20     @FXML
21     public void createNewTransaction()
            throws GeneralSecurityException {
22         Base64.Decoder decoder = Base64.getDecoder();
23         Signature signing =
                   Signature.getInstance("SHA256withDSA");
24         Integer ledgerId = BlockchainData.getInstance()
               .getTransactionLedgerFX().get(0).getLedgerId();
```

```
25          byte[] sendB = decoder.decode(toAddress.getText());
26          Transaction transaction =
                  new Transaction(WalletData.getInstance()
27                  .getWallet(),sendB ,Integer.parseInt(
                        value.getText()), ledgerId, signing);
28          BlockchainData.getInstance()
                  .addTransaction(transaction,false);
29          BlockchainData.getInstance()
                  .addTransactionState(transaction);
30      }
31  }
```

As you can see, it follows a similar design pattern. It contains only fields and methods referenced in the view and annotates them appropriately. Let's explain the code in the `createNewTransaction()` method. Lines 22 and 23 instantiate objects from our helper classes. Line 24 retrieves the current `ledgerId` at the time of clicking the button. On line 25 we use our Base64 object to convert our address from a string back into a byte array so that lines 26 and 27 can use it to create a new transaction. On line 28 we call on our service layer to add this transaction to the current block in the database. On line 29 we call on our service layer to adjust the current application state to include this transaction.

4.4 Summary

In this chapter, we covered how to create our front-end UI with its corresponding controllers. We learned how to use Scene Builder to create quick mock-ups of our scenes and create references for the back end. We learned how to create controller classes and how to design them properly. This is a small recap of what concepts we covered so far:

- Creation of FXML files using Scene Builder
- Creation of object and method references between the front and back ends of our application
- Creation of controller classes using `java` and `javafx`
- Setting up the Base64 external library encoder and its use
- Design of controller classes with separation of concerns in mind
- Creating dialog panes in `javafx`

CHAPTER 5

Setting Up the Network and Multithreading

"Networked" by Filip Rizov

S. Buzharovski, *Introducing Blockchain with Java*,
https://doi.org/10.1007/978-1-4842-7927-4_5

This chapter will cover creating our network layer; we will explain the creation and functionality of each of our multiple threads and how they fit into our application. Here we will explain the need for each thread and how some of them are used to create a peer-to-peer network where we transfer blockchain data and reach block consensus. In this chapter, we will be using the standard Java and Javafx libraries, which will help you learn every detail of the implementation. Before starting with this chapter, if you are unfamiliar with the topic of Java threads, you can find a quick tutorial that will help you grasp the basic concepts at `https://www.javatpoint.com/thread-concept-in-java`.

5.1 UI Thread

Since in our previous chapter we talked about the creation of our UI, let's start first with our UI thread. The object of the UI thread is for it to load the UI and then wait and listen for any user interaction. To make our UI responsive, our UI thread will need to be actively listening for user input. To allow the UI thread to wait and listen, we will have to move any continuous operations such as mining or sending requests to peers into other threads. This thread is fairly simple, and it mostly contains some standard boilerplate code from the `javafx` package. Let's look at the following code snippet:

```
1  package com.company.Threads;
2
3  import javafx.application.Application;
4  import javafx.fxml.FXMLLoader;
5  import javafx.scene.Parent;
6  import javafx.scene.Scene;
7  import javafx.stage.Stage;
8
```

```
9  import java.io.IOException;
10
11 public class UI extends Application {
12
13     @Override
14     public void start(Stage stage) {
15         Parent root = null;
16         try {
17             root = FXMLLoader.load(getClass()
               .getResource("../View/MainWindow.fxml"));
18         } catch (IOException e) {
19             e.printStackTrace();
20         }
21         stage.setTitle("E-Coin");
22         stage.setScene(new Scene(root, 900, 700));
23         stage.show();
24     }
25 }
```

Since we will be running the javafx application stage object in this thread, we will actually extend the Application class thread from the javafx.application package instead of the standard Thread class from the java.lang library. In this thread, we just need to override the start method and insert the rest of the logic inside it. The stage object will be passed from our main ECoin thread. On line 17, we set the root path by using the relative folder path from the location of our UI thread to the location of the first screen we want to see, which in our case is MainWindow.fxml. Lines 21–23 are used to set and display the initial scene of the UI. The location of our UI and all the other threads are in the Threads folder, as shown in Figure 5-1.

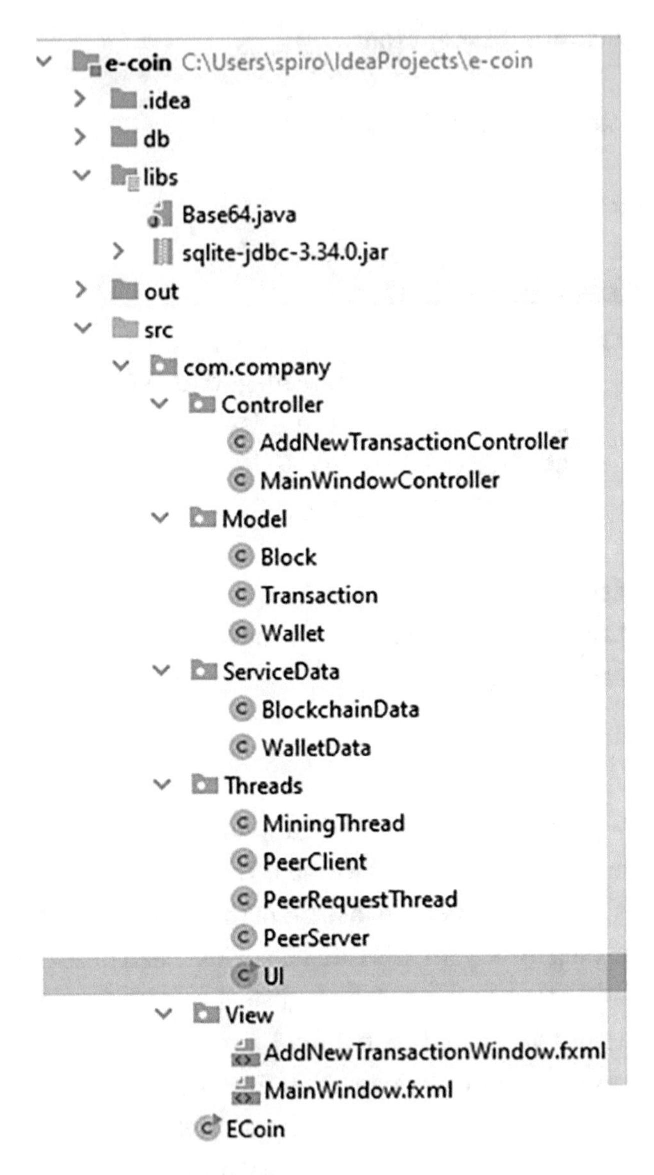

Figure 5-1. *The Threads folder*

5.2 Mining Thread

The object of our mining thread is for it to handle all the mining operations of the application. It will need to run continuously as long as our application is running and make sure new blocks are created at the appropriate interval. Also, since we will be using mining points as a method of achieving block consensus, this thread will also need to keep track of the points. Our mining thread will first check if we have a blockchain that is current and up-to-date, and then it will initiate the mining of a new block at a precise interval. This thread will loop every two seconds continuously.

Let's look at the code of our MiningThread class in our next code snippet:

```
1  package com.company.Threads;
2
3  import com.company.ServiceData.BlockchainData;
4
5  import java.time.LocalDateTime;
6  import java.time.ZoneOffset;
7
8  public class MiningThread extends Thread {
9
10     @Override
11     public void run() {
12         while (true) {
13             long lastMinedBlock = LocalDateTime.parse(
                   BlockchainData.getInstance()
14                     .getCurrentBlockChain().getLast()
                       .getTimeStamp())
                       .toEpochSecond(ZoneOffset.UTC);
```

```
15              if ((lastMinedBlock + BlockchainData
                        .getTimeoutInterval()) <
                        LocalDateTime.now().toEpochSecond(
                        ZoneOffset.UTC)) {
16                  System.out.println("BlockChain is too old for
                        mining! Update it from peers");
17              } else if ( ((lastMinedBlock + BlockchainData
                        .getMiningInterval()) - LocalDateTime
                        .now().toEpochSecond(ZoneOffset
                        .UTC)) > 0 ) {
18                  System.out.println("BlockChain is current,
                    mining will commence in " +
19                          ((lastMinedBlock + BlockchainData
                            .getMiningInterval()) -
                            LocalDateTime.now()
                            .toEpochSecond(ZoneOffset.UTC) ) +
                            " seconds");
20              } else {
21                  System.out.println("MINING NEW BLOCK");
22                      BlockchainData.getInstance().mineBlock();
23                      System.out.println(BlockchainData
                            .getInstance().getWalletBallanceFX());
24              }
25              System.out.println(LocalDateTime
                    .parse(BlockchainData.getInstance()
26                  .getCurrentBlockChain().getLast()
                    .getTimeStamp()).toEpochSecond(ZoneOffset.UTC));
27              try {
28                  Thread.sleep(2000);
29                  if (BlockchainData.getInstance()
                        .isExit()) { break; }
```

```
30                  BlockchainData.getInstance().setMiningPoints(
                         BlockchainData.getInstance()
                        .getMiningPoints() + 2);
31              } catch (InterruptedException e) {
32                  e.printStackTrace();
33              }
34          }
35      }
36 }
```

Our MiningThread class extends the Thread class from the java.lang package. We are overriding the run() method to set the logic that this thread will run on. On line 12 we are setting a while loop with a true parameter, which means we will be repeating the actions of this method as long as our application is running. On lines 13 and 14 we are setting a field with the value of the date when we mined our last block in seconds. For this purpose we are using the BlockchainData class, which is part of our service layer that we explain how to create in our next chapter. In order not to burden the code, our application won't handle different time zones; therefore, we will be using the standard ZoneOffset.UTC constant. Our first if statement on line 15 checks to see if more than 65 seconds (the timeout interval we have set up in our BlockchainData class that we will cover in Chapter 6) have passed since our last mined block. This will mean that our blockchain is too old, so there is no point in trying to mine it until we get an up-to-date version. Therefore, in this case, we print the message on line 16 in the console. If our first if statement is false, then on line 17 our else if statement checks to see if less than 60 seconds (the mining interval also covered in Chapter 6) have passed since the last mined block. If this is true, then we will print to the console the time remaining until we get to 60 seconds. If we reach our else statement on line 20, that means we are in that time window between 60 and 65 seconds since our last mined block and it's time to mine (create) another. Line 22 uses the service layer again to call a method to mine another block, and line 23 is used to print our new wallet balance to the console by using the service layer again. On lines 25 and 26, regardless of the outcome of the previous control flow statements, we print out the time of our last mined block to the console just for clarity. Since there is no point in this thread to loop as fast as it can on line 28, we call the thread to sleep for two seconds, which effectively makes this thread repeat every two seconds. We will set the rate of acquiring mining points to be one point per second; therefore, on line 29 we will add two mining points for each two seconds we wait.

EXERCISE 5-1

Try to come up with an even more efficient way of looping this thread.

Hint Try using the `Thread.sleep` method in multiple places with different times.

Note Make sure to maintain the same rate of acquiring mining points.

5.3 P2P Network Threads

Our next subsections will explain the classes that will create the threads for our peer-to-peer network to run. For us to create a peer-to-peer network, we will need our application to both act as a client and send requests to other peers and act as a server where it listens for requests from other peers and serves them. Let's start first with our `PeerClient` class thread.

For the purposes of our book, we won't be exposing our network to the Internet due to security concerns; instead, we will set different local ports to act as if they are different peers on our network.

5.3.1 PeerClient Thread

Our PeerClient thread will cycle through a predetermined list of peers and try to share our blockchain with them. Let's look at our next code snippet:

```
1  package com.company.Threads;
2
3  import com.company.Model.Block;
4  import com.company.ServiceData.BlockchainData;
5
6  import java.io.IOException;
7  import java.io.ObjectInputStream;
8  import java.io.ObjectOutputStream;
9  import java.net.Socket;
10 import java.net.SocketTimeoutException;
11 import java.util.LinkedList;
12 import java.util.Queue;
13 import java.util.concurrent.ConcurrentLinkedQueue;
14
15 public class PeerClient extends Thread {
16
17     private Queue<Integer> queue = new ConcurrentLinkedQueue<>();
18
19     public PeerClient() {
20         this.queue.add(6001);
21         this.queue.add(6002);
22     }
23
```

Before we override the `run()` method, we have a queue field that will be populated with the port numbers of the peers we want to connect to. As you can see on lines 19–21, we use the constructor to populate our queue with a few predetermined port numbers. We mentioned before that we will be using our local ports as peers. This means that instead of changing the IP address to connect to different peers, we will be using our local IP address 127.0.0.1 and instead change the local ports to which we connect.

EXERCISE 5-2

Try to use what we have learned so far to create a database table to store the list of ports instead of having them hard-coded here.

For extra points: Try using the `init()` method from our `ECoin` class to set everything up programmatically instead of manually doing it with the SQLite browser.

Let's move on to the next code snippet where we explore the `run()` method of this thread:

```
24      @Override
25      public void run() {
26          while (true) {
27              try (Socket socket = new Socket("127.0.0.1",
                     queue.peek())) {
28                  System.out.println("Sending blockchain object on
                     port: " + queue.peek());
29                  queue.add(queue.poll());
30                  socket.setSoTimeout(5000);
31
```

```
32                  ObjectOutputStream objectOutput =
                          new ObjectOutputStream(
                          socket.getOutputStream());
33                  ObjectInputStream objectInput =
                          new ObjectInputStream(
                          socket.getInputStream());
34
35                  LinkedList<Block> blockChain = BlockchainData
                        .getInstance().getCurrentBlockChain();
36                  objectOutput.writeObject(blockChain);
37
38                  LinkedList<Block> returnedBlockchain =
                        (LinkedList<Block>) objectInput
                        .readObject();
39                  System.out.println(" RETURNED BC LedgerId = " +
                        returnedBlockchain.getLast()
                        .getLedgerId()  +
40                        " Size= " + returnedBlockchain.getLast()
                        .getTransactionLedger().size());
41                  BlockchainData.getInstance()
                        .getBlockchainConsensus(
                        returnedBlockchain);
42                  Thread.sleep(2000);
43
44              } catch (SocketTimeoutException e) {
45                  System.out.println("The socket timed out");
46                  queue.add(queue.poll());
47              } catch (IOException e) {
48                  System.out.println("Client Error: " +
                          e.getMessage() + " -- Error on port: " +
                          queue.peek());
49                  queue.add(queue.poll());
```

```
50              } catch (InterruptedException |
                ClassNotFoundException e) {
51                  e.printStackTrace();
52                  queue.add(queue.poll());
53              }
54          }
55      }
56 }
```

Since we intend to constantly contact other peers and share our blockchain, we loop this thread in a continuous `while` loop just like our mining thread. Let's look at our `try` with resources first. We start by instantiating a socket with our local IP and the first port number in our queue. Next we print out a message in our console just to log the action, and on line 29 we move our port number that we used to instantiate this socket to the end of the queue. On the next line we also set a socket timeout. On lines 32 and 33 we instantiate our `ObjectOutputStream` and `ObjectInputStream` objects. We'll basically use the methods supplied by these objects to send our blockchain and then receive a response blockchain. On line 35 we use our service layer methods to get our blockchain object, and on the next line we use `objectOutput` to send our blockchain object to our peer. At this point, the blockchain we sent will be checked and compared by our peer with his local blockchain. When that process is done, our peer will send back the winning blockchain according to his consensus method. We retrieve this blockchain using our `objectInput` on line 38. However, since we don't really trust our peer, we run it through our consensus algorithm on the next line. Any peer can change the application on his local machine to try to send false information. That's why we run our consensus algorithm to validate the blockchain that we have received before, assuming it comes from a good actor. This way the good actors will keep spreading and extending the correct blockchain while stopping any attempts to share a false blockchain.

We will go into detail and explain our consensus algorithm and the steps we undertake in validating blockchains in the next chapter when we talk about the service layer. On line 40 we make our thread sleep for two seconds before looping again and attempting to connect to the next peer. Lastly in this method it's also important to look at our `catch` blocks. So far we send the port number to the back of the queue only after we successfully connect to the peer. However, in case we fail to connect to this peer, we also include statements in our `catch` blocks that send the current port number to the back of the queue. This makes sure we don't get stuck trying to connect to a single peer.

Important! Remember that no peer should trust another.

5.3.2 PeerServer Thread

Now it's time to look at the side that responds to the requests of other peers. The `PeerServer` thread listens on a certain port for incoming client requests from the other peers' `PeerClient` threads. In our implementation, we will open a separate `PeerRequestThread` for each incoming request. This will allow us to deal with multiple requests at once. Let's look at the following code snippet:

```
1  package com.company.Threads;
2
3
4  import java.io.IOException;
5  import java.net.ServerSocket;
6
7
```

```
8  public class PeerServer extends Thread {
9
10     private ServerSocket serverSocket;
11     public PeerServer(Integer socketPort) throws IOException {
12         this.serverSocket = new ServerSocket(socketPort);
13     }
14
15     @Override
16     public void run() {
17         while (true) {
18             try {
19                 new PeerRequestThread(
                           serverSocket.accept()).start();
20             } catch (IOException ex) {
21                 ex.printStackTrace();
22             }
23         }
24     }
25 }
```

On lines 10 to 12 we declare a ServerSocket and set up our constructor to assign the socketPort for our server. This is the port on which our server will listen to requests. Inside our run() method we set a continuous cycle where for each request that arrives at our server socket we create a new PeerRequestThread to handle that request. This way our server thread will always be available for new incoming requests.

5.4 PeerRequestThread

The PeerRequestThread handles each specific request that arrives at our peer. Let's look at the following code snippet and explain how it works:

```
1 package com.company.Threads;
2
3
4  import com.company.Model.Block;
5  import com.company.ServiceData.BlockchainData;
6
7  import java.io.IOException;
8  import java.io.ObjectInputStream;
9  import java.io.ObjectOutputStream;
10 import java.net.Socket;
11 import java.util.LinkedList;
12
13
14 public class PeerRequestThread extends Thread {
15
16    private Socket socket;
17
18    public PeerRequestThread(Socket socket) {
19        this.socket = socket;
20    }
21
22    @Override
23    public void run() {
24        try {
25
26            ObjectOutputStream objectOutput = new
                  ObjectOutputStream(socket
                          .getOutputStream());
27            ObjectInputStream objectInput = new
                      ObjectInputStream(socket
                          .getInputStream());
28
```

```
29              LinkedList<Block> recievedBC = (LinkedList<Block>)
                                    objectInput.readObject();
30              System.out.println("LedgerId = " +
                    recievedBC.getLast().getLedgerId() +
31                  " Size= " + recievedBC.getLast()
                    .getTransactionLedger().size());
32              objectOutput.writeObject(BlockchainData
                    .getInstance().getBlockchainConsensus(
                    recievedBC));
33          } catch (IOException | ClassNotFoundException ex) {
34              ex.printStackTrace();
35          }
36      }
37 }
```

We need to declare a socket and a constructor that will accept a socket from the PeerServer class as this thread is created. This socket is the link to the peer that sent the request. Our run() method is simple; on lines 26 and 27 we instantiate ObjectOutputStream and ObjectInputStream objects using the socket we received from the PeerServer. Recall that in our PeerClient class we are sending a LinkedList<Block> object in the request that contains the blockchain of that peer. On line 29 we use our objectInput class to instantiate the sent blockchain and name it receivedBC. Lines 30 and 31 simply log some information from the receivedBC. Lastly, on line 32, we use the objectOutput to send back the winning blockchain after we run the receivedBC through our blockchain consensus algorithm. You will notice that the method we call from the service layer is the same method we called in the PeerClient class when we received the response. In other words, when it comes to verifying incoming blockchains and reaching consensus between that one and the local one, the algorithm we use is ultimately the same regardless of whether it comes as a request or is received as a response.

5.5 Summary

In this chapter, we covered the creation of multiple threads that will allow our application to run responsively and uninterrupted. We learned how to use sockets to send and receive requests to other peers. We learned what elements are required to form a peer-to-peer network. We learned how to run the UI of our application, and we learned how to set up a mining subroutine. This is a small recap of what concepts we covered so far:

- Creating threads
- Using threads to handle different operations that need to run in parallel
- Creating and using network sockets
- Setting up network client and server threads
- Designing a peer-to-peer network
- Using the `javafx` application thread

CHAPTER 6

Service Layer

"Layered" by Filip Rizov

S. Buzharovski, *Introducing Blockchain with Java*,
https://doi.org/10.1007/978-1-4842-7927-4_6

This chapter will cover creating our service layer that will provide the functionality to everything covered in the previous chapters. In this chapter, we will finally implement all the methods that we briefly mentioned in our previous chapters. This chapter will most likely be the most complex one to grasp so far since it will try to tie together all the separate elements of our app. We recommend a solid familiarity with the previous chapters before continuing with this one.

6.1 WalletData

In this section, we will explain our `WalletData` class. It is used to store our wallet while our application is running and to make it available to every other part of our application. Any additional functionality of the wallet should be implemented through this class.

For now let's explain the following code:

```
1  package com.company.ServiceData;
2
3  import com.company.Model.Wallet;
4
5  import java.security.KeyFactory;
6  import java.security.NoSuchAlgorithmException;
7  import java.security.PrivateKey;
8  import java.security.PublicKey;
9  import java.security.spec.InvalidKeySpecException;
10 import java.security.spec.PKCS8EncodedKeySpec;
11 import java.security.spec.X509EncodedKeySpec;
12 import java.sql.*;
13
14 public class WalletData {
15
```

```
16      private Wallet wallet;
17      //singleton class
18      private static WalletData instance;
19
20      static {
21          instance = new WalletData();
22      }
23
24      public static WalletData getInstance() {
25          return instance;
26      }
```

First we start with the regular class imports. Then, since we will be storing our wallet in this class, we have a field of the `Wallet` class on line 16. Now because we want the same wallet to be available throughout the application we will create this class as a singleton class. Singleton is a basic design pattern, and it means that this class will be present only as a single object in memory and that we won't be able to instantiate any additional objects. This means there will be no chance of wallet duplicates all over our application. We make our class a singleton class by having a static field of our `WalletData` class, as shown on line 18, and then initiating it statically, as shown on lines 20–22. The last thing to mention is the `getInstance()` method. Instead of trying to instantiate new objects, we use this method to gain access to the class. Let's look at our next code snippet and explain the rest of the code contained in this class:

```
27
28      //This will load your wallet from the database.
29      public void loadWallet() throws SQLException,
              NoSuchAlgorithmException, InvalidKeySpecException {
```

```
30          Connection walletConnection = DriverManager
            .getConnection(
31                  "jdbc:sqlite:C:\\Users\\spiro\\IdeaProjects\\
                    e-coin\\db\\wallet.db");
32          Statement walletStatment = walletConnection
                    .createStatement();
33          ResultSet resultSet;
34          resultSet = walletStatment.executeQuery(
                    " SELECT * FROM WALLET ");
35          KeyFactory keyFactory = KeyFactory.getInstance("DSA");
36          PublicKey pub2 = null;
37          PrivateKey prv2 = null;
38          while (resultSet.next()) {
39              pub2 = keyFactory.generatePublic(
40                      new X509EncodedKeySpec(resultSet
                    .getBytes("PUBLIC_KEY")));
41              prv2 = keyFactory.generatePrivate(
42                      new PKCS8EncodedKeySpec(resultSet
                    .getBytes("PRIVATE_KEY")));
43          }
44          this.wallet = new Wallet(pub2, prv2);
45      }
46
47      public Wallet getWallet() {
48          return wallet;
49      }
50 }
51
```

First we have our `loadWallet()` method. We use it as the name suggests to load our wallet from the database. If you recall, we use this method in our application's `init()` method in the `ECoin` class to load our wallet.

Lines 30–34 are regular JDBC code for establishing a connection to the database where we keep our wallet keys and executing a select query to retrieve them. On line 35, we initiate our KeyFactory helper class. It's a class from the java.security package, and it will help us create the PublicKey and PrivateKey objects. On lines 36 and 37 we declare the PublicKey and PrivateKey objects. On lines 39 and 40 we use the KeyFactory helper class to generate a public key by inserting the byte array that we retrieve from the database. However, since the generatePublic(KeySpec ks) accepts a KeySpec object instead of byte array, we have to create a KeySpec object by constructing it from the X509EncodedKeySpec constructor. This class's parent class implements the KeySpec interface, which means we can use it to generate our public key, but also this class's constructor accepts our byte array, as shown in Figure 6-1.

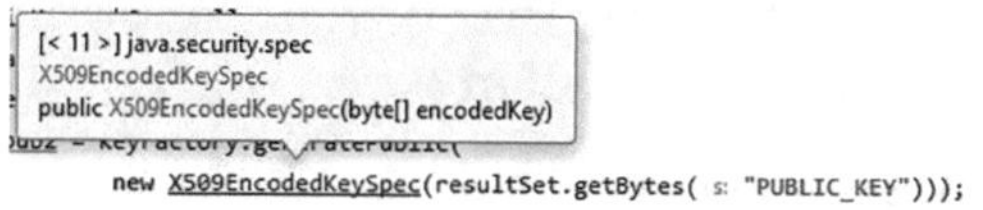

```
[< 11 >] java.security.spec
X509EncodedKeySpec
public X509EncodedKeySpec(byte[] encodedKey)
        new X509EncodedKeySpec(resultSet.getBytes( s: "PUBLIC_KEY")));
```

Figure 6-1. *X509EncodedKeySpec Class*

Lines 41 and 42 generate the private key for us using a similar method and the PKCS8EncodedKeySpec class. It also accepts a byte array and builds an object that implements the KeySpec interface, as shown in Figure 6-2.

```
[< 11 >] java.security.spec
PKCS8EncodedKeySpec
public PKCS8EncodedKeySpec(byte[] encodedKey)
        new PKCS8EncodedKeySpec(resultSet.
```

Figure 6-2. *PKCS8EncodedKeySpec class*

Both of these classes come from the java.security package, which is a great asset since we can use them right away. The last thing that we do is on line 44 where we create a new wallet object using our public and private keys we retrieved from the database and assign it to the wallet field in our class.

Our last method in this class is the getWallet() method, as shown on line 47. It's a simple getter method that we use to get the wallet object to the rest of our application.

6.2 BlockchainData

This is the biggest and most complex class in our application. Here we can find all the functionality regarding our blockchain. Let's start by showing all the imports in the next code snippet for reference:

```
1  package com.company.ServiceData;
2
3  import com.company.Model.Block;
4  import com.company.Model.Transaction;
5  import com.company.Model.allet;
6  import javafx.collections.FXCollections;
7  import javafx.collections.ObservableList;
8  import sun.security.provider.DSAPublicKeyImpl;
9
10 import java.security.*;
11 import java.sql.*;
12 import java.time.LocalDateTime;
13 import java.time.ZoneOffset;
14 import java.util.ArrayList;
15 import java.util.Arrays;
16 import java.util.Comparator;
17 import java.util.LinkedList;
18
```

Next let's go over the fields used in this class, as shown in our next code snippet:

```
18
19 public class BlockchainData {
20
21     private ObservableList<Transaction> newBlockTransactionsFX;
22     private ObservableList<Transaction> newBlockTransactions;
23     private LinkedList<Block> currentBlockChain =
               new LinkedList<>();
24     private Block latestBlock;
25     private boolean exit = false;
26     private int miningPoints;
27     private static final int TIMEOUT_INTERVAL = 65;
28     private static final int MINING_INTERVAL = 60;
29     //helper class.
30     private Signature signing = Signature
               .getInstance("SHA256withDSA");
31
32     //singleton class
33     private static BlockchainData instance;
34
```

On line 21 we have an `ObservableList` that contains `Transaction` objects. We are going to use this list only for displaying its contents on our front end. Next on line 22 we have an `ObservableList` that contains `Transaction` objects as well. This list will represent the current ledger of our blockchain. All the operations regarding our current ledger will be performed on this list. Our previous list will always be an exact copy of this list. On line 23 we finally have our current blockchain, which is represented as a `LinkedList` containing `Block` objects. Line 24 will represent our latest block that we are trying to add to the blockchain. On line 25 we have an `exit` Boolean that helps the `exit` command for our front-end work. Next on line 26 we have the mining points integer field that will help us keep track of our mining points that are used in our consensus algorithm. On lines 27 and 28 we have our mining and blockchain timeout interval constants. On line 30 we have the `Signature` helper class that helps us create signatures. On line 33 we have our `BlockchainData` as a static object, which helps us in making this a singleton class just like the `WalletData` class.

This is just a quick summary of the class fields; you will see how each one is used in more detail as we encounter them throughout the rest of this class.

In our next code snippet you will see the rest of the static initializer, the constructor, and the `getInstance()` method that we will use to create and access this singleton class:

```
34
35      static {
36          try {
37              instance = new BlockchainData();
38          } catch (NoSuchAlgorithmException e) {
39              e.printStackTrace();
40          }
41      }
42
43      public BlockchainData() throws NoSuchAlgorithmException {
44          newBlockTransactions = FXCollections
                .observableArrayList();
45          newBlockTransactionsFX = FXCollections
                .observableArrayList();
46      }
47
48      public static BlockchainData getInstance() {
49          return instance;
50      }
51
```

If you recall, we explained what these elements do in our previous section when we talked about the `WalletData` class. Let's look at the following code snippet:

```
51
52      Comparator<Transaction> transactionComparator = Comparator
                .comparing(Transaction::getTimestamp);
53      public ObservableList<Transaction>
        getTransactionLedgerFX() {
54          newBlockTransactionsFX.clear();
55          newBlockTransactions.sort(transactionComparator);
56          newBlockTransactionsFX.addAll(newBlockTransactions);
57          return FXCollections.observableArrayList(
                    newBlockTransactionsFX);
58      }
59
```

On lines 53 to 58 we have a simple method that is used for displaying our current transaction ledger. It simply transfers the transactions from our current ledger to an `ObservableList` that we can display on our UI. We do this simply to maintain a separation of concerns. The only other thing to mention is the `transactionComparator` on line 52, which sorts our transactions at the time of creation.

Let's move on to the next code snippet:

```
60      public String getWalletBallanceFX() {
61          return getBalance(currentBlockChain,
                    newBlockTransactions,
62                  WalletData.getInstance().getWallet()
                    .getPublicKey()).toString();
63      }
64
```

```
65      private Integer getBalance(LinkedList<Block> blockChain,
66                                  ObservableList<Transaction>
                    currentLedger, PublicKey walletAddress) {
67          Integer balance = 0;
68          for (Block block : blockChain) {
69              for (Transaction transaction : block
                    .getTransactionLedger()) {
70                  if (Arrays.equals(transaction
                        .getFrom(), walletAddress.getEncoded())) {
71                      balance -= transaction.getValue();
72                  }
73                  if (Arrays.equals(transaction
                        .getTo(), walletAddress.getEncoded())) {
74                      balance += transaction.getValue();
75                  }
76              }
77          }
78          for (Transaction transaction : currentLedger) {
79              if (Arrays.equals(transaction
                    .getFrom(), walletAddress.getEncoded())) {
80                  balance -= transaction.getValue();
81              }
82          }
83          return balance;
84      }
85
```

Let's start with the getBalance method on line 65 since it's used in the method on line 60. This method goes through a given blockchain and a current ledger with potential transactions for the new block and finds the balance for the given public address. This method is useful not only for displaying the current balance but also for verifying if a certain address has enough coins before sending them. On lines 65 and 66 we see the input parameters we just mentioned. On lines 68 to 77 we go through each block of the blockchain, and for each transaction we check whether the given address is sending or receiving funds. We also adjust the price accordingly.

To prevent double spending we also need to subtract any funds we are already trying to send that exist in the current transaction ledger. Remember that double spending is a situation where the sender tries to send his total funds multiple times, effectively multiplying his funds out of thin air. This happens on lines 78–82. If you are wondering why we don't count incoming funds until they are put on the blockchain, it's to prevent any bugs where an invalid incoming transaction is created just so that we can send the incoming funds before the consensus discovers and invalidates the incoming transaction. Finally, on line 83, we return the balance that we calculated.

Now if we go back to our first method on lines 60–63 we can see that it simply calls our getBalance method and inputs the local blockchain, the current ledger, and our wallet's public address. This method is used to retrieve our own current balance when we need it throughout the application.

Let's look at our next method displayed in the next code snippet:

```
86      private void verifyBlockChain(LinkedList<Block>
                    currentBlockChain) throws
                    GeneralSecurityException {
87          for (Block block : currentBlockChain) {
88              if (!block.isVerified(signing)) {
89                  throw new GeneralSecurityException(
                        "Block validation failed");
90              }
91              ArrayList<Transaction> transactions = block
                        .getTransactionLedger();
```

```
92                for (Transaction transaction : transactions) {
93                    if (!transaction.isVerified(signing)) {
94                        throw new GeneralSecurityException(
                                "Transaction validation failed");
95                    }
96                }
97            }
98        }
```

This is the method that actually checks the validity of each transaction and each block. In this method we can finally see the `isVerified` methods from the `Block` and `Transaction` classes in action and how they fit in our application. If you need, feel free to go back to Chapter 2 and recall how these methods worked. The method itself is simple: it goes through all of the blocks and all of the transactions within each block and checks if each one is valid. You can see further in our book that this method is used to validate our own blockchain as well as validate a blockchain we have received from other peers.

Now let's move on to the next code snippet:

```
99        public void addTransactionState(Transaction transaction) {
100           newBlockTransactions.add(transaction);
101           newBlockTransactions.sort(transactionComparator);
102       }
103
104       public void addTransaction(Transaction transaction,
              boolean blockReward) throws GeneralSecurityException {
105           try {
106               if (getBalance(currentBlockChain,
                      newBlockTransactions,
107                   new DSAPublicKeyImpl(transaction.getFrom())
                      ) < transaction.getValue() && !blockReward) {
108                   throw new GeneralSecurityException("Not enough
```

```
                funds by sender to record transaction");
109             } else {
110                 Connection connection = DriverManager
                    .getConnection
111                         ("jdbc:sqlite:C:\\Users\\spiro
                    \\IdeaProjects\\e-coin\\db\\blockchain.db");
112
113                 PreparedStatement pstmt;
114                 pstmt = connection.prepareStatement("INSERT
                    INTO TRANSACTIONS" +
115                         "(\"FROM\", \"TO\", LEDGER_ID, VALUE,
                         SIGNATURE, CREATED_ON) " +
116                         " VALUES (?,?,?,?,?,?) ");
117                 pstmt.setBytes(1, transaction.getFrom());
118                 pstmt.setBytes(2, transaction.getTo());
119                 pstmt.setInt(3, transaction.getLedgerId());
120                 pstmt.setInt(4, transaction.getValue());
121                 pstmt.setBytes(5, transaction.getSignature());
122                 pstmt.setString(6, transaction.getTimestamp());
123                 pstmt.executeUpdate();
124
125                 pstmt.close();
126                 connection.close();
127             }
128         } catch (SQLException e) {
129             System.out.println("Problem with DB: " +
                e.getMessage());
130             e.printStackTrace();
131         }
132
133     }
134
```

On lines 99–102 you will find our `addTransactionState` method. It's a simple method that adds a given transaction into our current transaction ledger and sorts it. If you recall, we have already mentioned this method in our `init()` application method and in our `AddNewTransactionController` class.

Now let's look at the `addTransaction` method. The general idea of this method as its name suggests is to add a new transaction to our ledger. This method will take a `Transaction` object and a Boolean flag marking if it's a reward transaction for the miner or it's a regular transaction. We'll dive deeper into where and how we use this reward transaction when we talk about our `mineBlock()` method later in this chapter. One thing to note, though, is that in our blockchain the reward transactions create new coins and award them to the miner that mines that block, so we make sure to flag this transactions in order to skip the coin balance check performed by our `getBalance` method.

Important! Note that different blockchains have different implementations regarding if their total coins are capped or uncapped and how they are rewarded to the miners. Our way is just one way of doing it.

Let's go back to our method and look at lines 106–109. You can notice that we perform a check calling the `getBalance` method and check if the sender has more coins than the transaction's amount. This of course makes sure we reject any transaction that tries to cheat and send more money than the sender actually has. However, also notice the caveat at the end where we use the reward transaction flag to skip this check if this is a reward transaction. If we don't do this, the reward transactions will otherwise fail this check because the `getBalance` method will discover that these coins appear out of thin air. Since this feature is intended in order to reward miners, the need to skip the `getBalance` method when it comes to reward transactions is by now apparent. Next in our method we see that if the check to invalidate the transaction fails, then we move on to actually add it to our ledger. Lines 110 until the end use JDBC to add the transaction to our database as well. Remember that we have covered similar operations using JDBC when we explained our application's `init` method in Chapter 3 in case you need to recall how this part of the code works.

EXERCISE 6-1

If you are familiar with any ORM solutions like Hibernate, you can try to implement it here to automatically add the transaction in the database instead of doing it manually like we do in our `addTransaction` method.

Let's move on to our next method `loadTransactionLedger`. This method is used within the `loadBlockchain()` method as a means to load the transaction ledger for each block from the database to the application.

Let's look at the following code snippet:

```
171
172     private ArrayList<Transaction> loadTransactionLedger(
                             Integer ledgerID) throws SQLException {
173         ArrayList<Transaction> transactions = new ArrayList<>();
174         try {
175             Connection connection = DriverManager.getConnection
176                     ("jdbc:sqlite:C:\\Users\\
                    spiro\\IdeaProjects\\e-coin\\db\\
                    blockchain.db");
177             PreparedStatement stmt = connection.prepareStatement
178                     (" SELECT  * FROM TRANSACTIONS WHERE
                    LEDGER_ID = ?");
```

```
179             stmt.setInt(1, ledgerID);
180             ResultSet resultSet = stmt.executeQuery();
181             while (resultSet.next()) {
182                 transactions.add(new Transaction(
183                         resultSet.getBytes("FROM"),
184                         resultSet.getBytes("TO"),
185                         resultSet.getInt("VALUE"),
186                         resultSet.getBytes("SIGNATURE"),
187                         resultSet.getInt("LEDGER_ID"),
188                         resultSet.getString("CREATED_ON")
189                 ));
190             }
191             resultSet.close();
192             stmt.close();
193             connection.close();
194         } catch (SQLException e) {
195             e.printStackTrace();
196         }
197         return transactions;
198     }
199
```

This method retrieves and returns a list of `Transaction` objects from the database. It takes an integer as a parameter, which signifies the ledger ID that we use to retrieve only the transactions for the required ledger. Lines 175 to 180 are standard JDBC where we establish a connection to the database, create our statement, insert the ledger ID as part of the query statement, and execute the query. Lines 181–190 cycle through the result set, create a new transaction for each result, and add it to the transactions `ArrayList`. The rest of the method is just closing connections and the return statement, which returns the list of transactions we have just retrieved from the database.

Now let's go back to the loadBlockChain() method, which we briefly mentioned when explaining the use of loadTransactionLedger. This method is used whenever we want to load the whole blockchain from our database and set up the state of the app accordingly. If you recall, this method is used in the application's init method, and also you will see it used in a few cases later in this chapter when we talk about the consensus algorithm. The method is quite large, so we will split it into the next two code snippets:

```
135    public void loadBlockChain() {
136        try {
137            Connection connection = DriverManager.getConnection
138                    ("jdbc:sqlite:C:\\Users\\spiro\\
                     IdeaProjects\\e-coin\\db\\blockchain.db");
139            Statement stmt = connection.createStatement();
140            ResultSet resultSet = stmt.executeQuery(" SELECT *
               FROM BLOCKCHAIN ");
141            while (resultSet.next()) {
142                this.currentBlockChain.add(new Block(
143                        resultSet.getBytes("PREVIOUS_HASH"),
144                        resultSet.getBytes("CURRENT_HASH"),
145                        resultSet.getString("CREATED_ON"),
146                        resultSet.getBytes("CREATED_BY"),
147                        resultSet.getInt("LEDGER_ID"),
148                        resultSet.getInt("MINING_POINTS"),
149                        resultSet.getDouble("LUCK"),
150                        loadTransactionLedger(
                           resultSet.getInt("LEDGER_ID"))
151                ));
152            }
153
```

Lines 137–140 are pretty standard JDBC code. We set up the connection to our database and create and execute our query to select everything from the BLOCKCHAIN table. Next we cycle through the result set creating a new Block object and adding it to the currentBlockChan field from this class. One thing to note is line 150 where we use the loadTransactionLedger method with the current ledger ID from the result set to retrieve the list of transactions for this block and include it in the Block object's constructor. Let's move on to the second part of this method:

```
153
154             latestBlock = currentBlockChain.getLast();
155             Transaction transaction = new Transaction(
                        new Wallet(),
156                     WalletData.getInstance().getWallet()
                        .getPublicKey().getEncoded(),
157                     100, latestBlock.getLedgerId() + 1,
                        signing);
158             newBlockTransactions.clear();
159             newBlockTransactions.add(transaction);
160             verifyBlockChain(currentBlockChain);
161             resultSet.close();
162             stmt.close();
163             connection.close();
164         } catch (SQLException | NoSuchAlgorithmException e) {
165             System.out.println("Problem with DB: " +
                                     e.getMessage());
166             e.printStackTrace();
167         } catch (GeneralSecurityException e) {
168             e.printStackTrace();
169         }
170     }
171
```

In this part of the method, we will update the state of the application so that it works properly from this point onward. To achieve this, we will need to change our latestBlock and newBlockTransactions fields. On line 154 we set up the lastestBlock field by getting the last block from our currentBlockChain list, which got filled up in the first part of this method. Next, to set up our newBlocksTransactions list first, we create a new reward transaction object on lines 155–157. Then we clear the list and add the new transaction we just created. This is the reward transaction for our future block. The last important line is line 160, where we can see the verifyBlockChain method on the currentBlockChain we just loaded from our database. This is an important step since it covers cases when we import someone else's database and we need to check its validity.

It's time to go over the methods that constitute the mining functionality. In our next code snippet, let's look briefly at the mineBlock() method.

```
200     public void mineBlock() {
201         try {
202             finalizeBlock(WalletData.getInstance()
                .getWallet());
203             addBlock(latestBlock);
204         } catch (SQLException | GeneralSecurityException e) {
205             System.out.println("Problem with DB: " +
                                   e.getMessage());
206             e.printStackTrace();
207         }
208     }
209
```

Let's first recall that this is the method we call in the MiningThread class when it's time to mine new block. This method simply calls the methods finalizeBlock and addBlock. The finalizeBlock method performs the necessary steps to finish up the latest block and adds it to our currentBlockChain list. Different miners can have different latest (nonfinal) blocks with different transactions in them. The addBlock method simply adds the block to the database.

Let's start explaining the finalizeBlock method first, as shown in the following code snippet:

```
209
210     private void finalizeBlock(Wallet minersWallet) throws
                    GeneralSecurityException, SQLException {
211         latestBlock = new Block(BlockchainData
                        .getInstance().currentBlockChain);
212         latestBlock.setTransactionLedger(new ArrayList<>(
                                 newBlockTransactions));
213         latestBlock.setTimeStamp(LocalDateTime.now()
            .toString());
214         latestBlock.setMinedBy(minersWallet.getPublicKey()
                                   .getEncoded());
215         latestBlock.setMiningPoints(miningPoints);
216         signing.initSign(minersWallet.getPrivateKey());
217         signing.update(latestBlock.toString().getBytes());
218         latestBlock.setCurrHash(signing.sign());
219         currentBlockChain.add(latestBlock);
220         miningPoints = 0;
221         //Reward transaction
222         latestBlock.getTransactionLedger()
                        .sort(transactionComparator);
223         addTransaction(latestBlock.getTransactionLedger()
                        .get(0), true);
224         Transaction transaction = new Transaction(new Wallet(),
                  minersWallet.getPublicKey().getEncoded(),
225               100, latestBlock.getLedgerId() + 1, signing);
```

```
226         newBlockTransactions.clear();
227         newBlockTransactions.add(transaction);
228     }
229
```

In this method, we start with preparing/finalizing our `latestBlock`. On line 211 we create a new `Block` and pass it to `latestBlock`. On line 212, we add our `newBlockTransactions` to the ledger of the `latestBlock`. On line 213, we set the timestamp to the current time. On line 214, we set our own wallet address since we are trying to mine this block as `minedBy`. On line 215, we set the current mining points we have accumulated. If you need to recall how we accumulate mining points, you can revisit the "Mining Thread" section in Chapter 5. By this point our `latestBlock` contains all the data except for the signature, which in this case will be set as the current hash. Let's recall that this signature actually represents an encoded value of all the data contained in our block. That is why we always create the signature and set the current hash last. Once this is done, any changes to the block will result in the block failing the verification since our signature when decoded with our public key won't match the present data in the block.

Important! If you need more help in understanding how we create and use the signature, revisit Chapter 2.

Next on line 219 we include the `latestBlock` into our `CurrentBlockChain` since we have finalized it completely. Before we finish this method, however, we need to set up a few more items. On line 220, we reset our mining points to 0. On line 222, we add the reward transaction of the block we just finalized to the database since until now we have kept it only in the `newBlockTransactions` list, which we copied in our `lastestBlock`. Once this is done, we create a new reward transaction object, we clear the newBlockTransactions list since it contains the old transactions of the block we already finalized, and we add the new reward transaction to our newBlockTransactions. The newBlockTransactions list, preloaded with the next reward transaction, is now ready to get filled up with new transactions until the next mining cycle. This reward transaction is what the miner gets for successfully mining the next block.

EXERCISE 6-2

Adding a reward transaction and keeping track of it looks a bit burdensome and redundant. Can you streamline the codebase so that we don't have to do this?

Hint We all know that the block's creator is the one getting rewarded. Try tweaking the getBalance method to add an extra 100 coins for each block that the address in question has created. This will remove the need for reward transaction to be added explicitly.

Now once we have finalized/mined our block, it's time to add it to the database as well. For this purpose, we mentioned that we use the addBlock method. Let's look at the following code snippet and explain it:

```
229
230     private void addBlock(Block block) {
231         try {
232             Connection connection = DriverManager.getConnection
233                     ("jdbc:sqlite:C:\\Users\\spiro\\
                     IdeaProjects\\e-coin\\db\\blockchain.db");
234             PreparedStatement pstmt;
```

```
235             pstmt = connection.prepareStatement
236                     ("INSERT INTO BLOCKCHAIN(PREVIOUS_HASH,
                        CURRENT_HASH, LEDGER_ID, CREATED_ON," +
237                     " CREATED_BY, MINING_POINTS, LUCK)
                        VALUES (?,?,?,?,?,?,?) ");
238             pstmt.setBytes(1, block.getPrevHash());
239             pstmt.setBytes(2, block.getCurrHash());
240             pstmt.setInt(3, block.getLedgerId());
241             pstmt.setString(4, block.getTimeStamp());
242             pstmt.setBytes(5, block.getMinedBy());
243             pstmt.setInt(6, block.getMiningPoints());
244             pstmt.setDouble(7, block.getLuck());
245             pstmt.executeUpdate();
246             pstmt.close();
247             connection.close();
248         } catch (SQLException e) {
249             System.out.println("Problem with DB: " +
                e.getMessage());
250             e.printStackTrace();
251         }
252     }
253
```

By now you should be well versed in executing JDBC queries. This method accepts a single `Block` object parameter and uses it to create a new entry inside our `BLOCKCHAIN` table in the database, which will represent our latest mined block. The last thing to note is that this `addBlock` method is also used in our next method that we are about to explain, which is `replaceBlockchainInDatabase`.

The need for this method arises when we need to replace our own blockchain with a blockchain we have received from another peer. We will cover these reasons when we go over the consensus algorithm right after we explain this method first. Let's look at the following code snippet:

```
254     private void replaceBlockchainInDatabase(LinkedList<Block>
        receivedBC) {
255         try {
256             Connection connection = DriverManager.getConnection
257                     ("jdbc:sqlite:C:\\Users\\spiro\\
                    IdeaProjects\\e-coin\\db\\blockchain.db");
258             Statement clearDBStatement = connection
                            .createStatement();
259             clearDBStatement.executeUpdate(" DELETE FROM
                BLOCKCHAIN ");
260             clearDBStatement.executeUpdate(" DELETE FROM
                TRANSACTIONS ");
261             clearDBStatement.close();
262             connection.close();
263             for (Block block : receivedBC) {
264                 addBlock(block);
265                 boolean rewardTransaction = true;
266                 block.getTransactionLedger()
                        .sort(transactionComparator);
267                 for (Transaction transaction : block
                        .getTransactionLedger()) {
268                     addTransaction(transaction,
                        rewardTransaction);
269                     rewardTransaction = false;
270                 }
271             }
```

```
272         } catch (SQLException | GeneralSecurityException e) {
273             System.out.println("Problem with DB: " +
                                   e.getMessage());
274             e.printStackTrace();
275         }
276     }
277
```

This method accepts a LinkedList<Block> object parameter, which represents a blockchain that we want to import into our database. The method starts by establishing a connection to our database and executes statements on lines 259 and 260 that clear the existing data in our tables. On lines 263–271, we cycle through the blocks and their transactions of the blockchain we want to import and call the addBlock and addTransaction methods we explained earlier to write each one to the database.

EXERCISE 6-3

Reusing the addBlock and addTransaction methods in the replaceBlockchainInDatabase method is not an efficient way of importing the blockchain to the database. Each call to one of these methods opens and closes a connection to the database. Can you write a more efficient implementation that serves the same purpose?

6.2.1 Blockchain Consensus Protocol

Finally we have arrived to the method that executes the consensus algorithm in our application. Before we start explaining the code, we need to talk a little bit about blockchain consensus.

Blockchain consensus, or, in other words, the network consensus regarding the blockchain that each peer builds and shares, is at the heart of this technology. The main problem that needs to be solved for the consensus to be reached reliably each time is the so-called Byzantine generals problem. The term takes its name from an allegory developed to describe a situation in which, to avoid catastrophic failure of the system, the system's actors must agree on a concerted strategy, but some of these actors are unreliable. In short, the byzantine generals problem goes like this: a number of Byzantine generals surround an enemy city and are trying to decide whether to attack or retreat. Whatever is decided, they must all follow the same decision. The problem gets more complicated by the fact that the generals are separated from each other, and they communicate only through messages. Also, some generals might be traitors and might try to spread misinformation to the other generals regarding their intentions to create even more confusion.

Let's circle back now and draw some parallels between the generals problem and our blockchain. The generals in question regarding our application will be the miners/peers. The need for consensus between them is obvious here; otherwise we end up with many different useless blockchains. Also, the ability of the good peers to discover and discard attempts at tampering with the validity of the blockchain by bad actors is mandatory. There is no use in reaching consensus on a blockchain filled with inaccuracies by bad actors. This means we have to treat each peer as potentially a bad actor and untrusted source.

To explore the many complexities and problems that consensus solutions face, we decided to implement our own slightly modified version of the bitcoin's proof-of-work algorithm. Our solution is of course far inferior to what bitcoin and other cryptocurrencies actually use, but we think that it will serve as a better learning tool to grasp the problems that consensus algorithms face.

```
277
278     public LinkedList<Block> getBlockchainConsensus(
                LinkedList<Block> receivedBC) {
279         try {
280             //Verify the validity of the received blockchain.
281             verifyBlockChain(receivedBC);
282             //Check if we have received an identical blockchain.
283             if (!Arrays.equals(receivedBC.getLast()
                    .getCurrHash(), getCurrentBlockChain().getLast()
                    .getCurrHash())) {
284                 if (checkIfOutdated(receivedBC) != null) {
285                     return getCurrentBlockChain();
286                 } else {
287                     if (checkWhichIsCreatedFirst(receivedBC)
                        != null) {
288                         return getCurrentBlockChain();
289                     } else {
290                         if (compareMiningPointsAndLuck(
                                receivedBC) != null) {
291                             return getCurrentBlockChain();
292                         }
293                     }
294                 }
295                 // if only the transaction ledgers are different
                    then combine them.
296             } else if (!receivedBC.getLast()
                        .getTransactionLedger().equals(
                        getCurrentBlockChain()
297                     .getLast().getTransactionLedger())) {
298                 updateTransactionLedgers(receivedBC);
299                 System.out.println("Transaction ledgers
                                        updated");
```

```
300                 return receivedBC;
301             } else {
302                 System.out.println("blockchains are identical");
303             }
304         } catch (GeneralSecurityException e) {
305             e.printStackTrace();
306         }
307         return receivedBC;
308     }
309
```

Our getBlockchainConsensus method accepts a LinkedList<Block> parameter, which will represent the blockchain that we have received from a peer. We will be performing validation checks and several comparisons between our local blockchain and the one we receive. First we will explain the overall logic of the method and then dive into each method that we still haven't explained. On line 281 we start by verifying the validity of the received blockchain. As we mentioned earlier, we don't trust any peer, so we always verify anything we get from them. If the method we received fails our validation check, the story ends there. Our application throws an exception, and we discard the received blockchain. If the received blockchain is verified, then we move on with comparison. On line 283 we perform our first comparison between our own method and the one we received. Here we check if the current hash of each blockchain is an exact match. This check will be true only if our blockchains match completely. Let's go over the case when our blockchains current hashes don't match. This means that both blockchains have different miners of the last block. When this happens, it means that it's time for us to perform some consensus checks to determine which miner gets to mine the last block.

Our first consensus check is to determine whether any of the blockchains are outdated, meaning checking if they are older than a full mining interval. We will explain the `checkIfOutdated` method in further detail later; for now we will just mention its functionality. It simply determines if any method is outdated and discards it. If the received one is outdated, then we keep using ours. If ours is outdated, we discard ours and use the received one from this point forward. If both are outdated, then we do nothing regarding consensus, and we wait to receive an up-to-date blockchain. If both are up-to-date, then we move on with the consensus checks.

Our next check is on line 287 and runs the method `checkWhichIsCreatedFirst`. This method is here to determine if both blockchains have the same initial block. If they don't, we will use the one that got created first. Our next check on line 290 is reached when both blockchains do have the same initial block. Here we run the method `compareMiningPointsAndLuck`. By the time we reach this method we have determined that the received blockchain is valid, and both blockchains are up-to-date and identical until the last block. To determine which blockchain's last block we are going to use, we will check each blockchain's recorded mining points. In case of a tie, we will determine the outcome by their recorded luck value, which is just a large random number.

Now let's move back to line 283 and go over the case when the blockchain's current hashes are identical. This means that the miner for the last block has already been determined in a previous run of this method. Recall from Chapter 5 that we constantly try to share our blockchain to other peers so this `getBlockchainConsensus` method gets run repeatedly. So if our current hashes are identical, we move on to line 296. On line 296 we compare the transaction ledgers of the blockchains. There are cases where we have determined the correct miner before we get all the transactions that happened during that block. Let's imagine a case where peer 1, peer 2, and peer 3 are trying to share their blockchains just after mining a new block. Peer 1 has the highest mining points, so we expect his blockchain to win the consensus checks with peer 2 and peer 3. However, all the peers start with only the transactions they have recorded on their blocks. First peer 1 shares his blockchain with peer 2, and peer 2 accepts peer 1's last block but also adds his transactions to the ones peer 2 already has. Next, peer 1 shares his blockchain with peer 3 and the same thing happens. At this point, both peer 2 and peer 3 contain peer 1's last block and his transactions. At this point, when peer 2 tries to share its blockchain with peer 3, they will both have the same current hashes since they both have peer 1's last block; however, peer 2 is missing peer 3's transactions and vice versa. This is the point at which the consensus algorithm reaches line 296 and checks their transaction ledgers. Since their transaction ledgers won't be identical, the method `updateTransactionLedgers` on line 298 will be called.

QUESTION 6-1

In the previous scenario, what will happen next if peer 3 tries to share his blockchain with peer 1?

QUESTION 6-2

In the previous scenario, what will happen next if peer 2 tries to share his blockchain with peer 3 again?

See the answers at the end of this chapter.

For the last case, when both blockchains are identical, then the message on line 302 gets printed in console, and the received blockchain gets returned on line 307.

Now let's circle back and go over the methods we mentioned. First we start with the checkIfOutdated method, as shown in the following snippet:

```
326
327     private LinkedList<Block> checkIfOutdated(
                LinkedList<Block> receivedBC) {
328         //Check how old the blockchains are.
329         long lastMinedLocalBlock = LocalDateTime.parse
330                 (getCurrentBlockChain().getLast()
                 .getTimeStamp())
                     .toEpochSecond(ZoneOffset.UTC);
331         long lastMinedRcvdBlock = LocalDateTime.parse
332                 (receivedBC.getLast().getTimeStamp())
                     .toEpochSecond(ZoneOffset.UTC);
333         //if both are old just do nothing
334         if ((lastMinedLocalBlock + TIMEOUT_INTERVAL) <
                LocalDateTime.now().toEpochSecond(
                ZoneOffset.UTC) &&
335                 (lastMinedRcvdBlock + TIMEOUT_INTERVAL) <
                    LocalDateTime.now().toEpochSecond(
                    ZoneOffset.UTC)) {
336             System.out.println("both are old check other
            peers");
337             //If your blockchain is old but the received one is
                    new use the received one
338         } else if ((lastMinedLocalBlock + TIMEOUT_INTERVAL) <
                LocalDateTime.now().toEpochSecond(
                ZoneOffset.UTC) &&
339                 (lastMinedRcvdBlock + TIMEOUT_INTERVAL) >=
            LocalDateTime.now().toEpochSecond(
            ZoneOffset.UTC)) {
```

```
340             //we reset the mining points since we weren't
                     contributing until now.
341             setMiningPoints(0);
342             replaceBlockchainInDatabase(receivedBC);
343             setCurrentBlockChain(new LinkedList<>());
344             loadBlockChain();
345             System.out.println("received blockchain won!,
                                  local BC was old");
346             //If received one is old but local is new send
                ours to them
347         } else if ((lastMinedLocalBlock + TIMEOUT_INTERVAL) >
                LocalDateTime.now().toEpochSecond(
                ZoneOffset.UTC) &&
348                 (lastMinedRcvdBlock + TIMEOUT_INTERVAL) <
                        LocalDateTime.now().toEpochSecond(
                        ZoneOffset.UTC)) {
349
350             return getCurrentBlockChain();
351         }
352         return null;
353     }
354
```

This method accepts the received blockchain as a parameter. We don't need to pass the local blockchain since we can access it from within this method. Lines 329–331 retrieve the creation times of the last blocks of both blockchains in seconds. Lines 334 and 335 check if both are outdated by comparing the last mined blocks in seconds and adding the timeout interval to the current time. If they both are outdated, the message on line 336 gets printed in the console, and the null on line 352 is returned. The next check on lines 338 and 339 checks if your local blockchain is outdated but the one you received is up-to-date. If this is the case, then the lines 341–345 run. This means that the mining points get reset since we were spending time with an outdated blockchain until now. Then we add the received blockchain to our database and set the application state to match. The method returns null in this case as well. Our last case happens when the check on lines 347 and 348 are true, which means that the receiving blockchain is old but our local is up-to-date. In this case, we return our local blockchain.

Our next method is the checkWhichIsCreatedFirst method.

```
355     private LinkedList<Block> checkWhichIsCreatedFirst(
             LinkedList<Block> receivedBC) {
356         //Compare timestamps to see which one is
            created first.
357         long initRcvBlockTime = LocalDateTime.parse(
            receivedBC.getFirst().getTimeStamp())
358                 .toEpochSecond(ZoneOffset.UTC);
359         long initLocalBlockTIme = LocalDateTime.parse(
                  getCurrentBlockChain().getFirst()
360                 .getTimeStamp()).toEpochSecond(
                    ZoneOffset.UTC);
361         if (initRcvBlockTime < initLocalBlockTIme) {
362             //we reset the mining points since we weren't
                contributing until now.
363             setMiningPoints(0);
364             replaceBlockchainInDatabase(receivedBC);
365             setCurrentBlockChain(new LinkedList<>());
366             loadBlockChain();
367             System.out.println("PeerClient blockchain won!,
                                  PeerServer's BC was old");
```

```
368         } else if (initLocalBlockTIme < initRcvBlockTime) {
369             return getCurrentBlockChain();
370         }
371         return null;
372     }
373
```

In this method, first we retrieve the creation times of the initial blocks in seconds, as shown on lines 357–360. On line 361 we check if the received blockchain's creation time in seconds is smaller than the one from our local blockchain. This means that the receiving blockchain got created first. If this is the case, then lines 363–367 execute, and the null on line 371 gets returned. If the case is the opposite, which means our local blockchain got created first, then we simply return our local blockchain.

Let's look at the compareMiningPointsAndLuck method in the following snippet:

```
374     private LinkedList<Block> compareMiningPointsAndLuck(
                LinkedList<Block> receivedBC)
375             throws GeneralSecurityException {
376         //check if both blockchains have the same prevHashes
            to confirm they are both
377         //contending to mine the last block
378         //if they are the same compare the mining points and
            luck in case of equal mining points
379         //of last block to see who wins
380         if (receivedBC.equals(getCurrentBlockChain())) {
381             //If received block has more mining points
                points or luck in case of tie
382             // transfer all transactions to the winning
                block and add them in DB.
```

```
383            if (receivedBC.getLast().getMiningPoints() >
                       getCurrentBlockChain()
384                    .getLast().getMiningPoints() ||
                       receivedBC.getLast().getMiningPoints()
385                    .equals(getCurrentBlockChain()
                       .getLast().getMiningPoints()) &&
386                    receivedBC.getLast().getLuck() >
                       getCurrentBlockChain().getLast()
                       .getLuck()) {
387                //remove the reward transaction from our
                   losing block and
388                // transfer the transactions to the
                   winning block
389                getCurrentBlockChain().getLast()
                  .getTransactionLedger().remove(0);
390                for (Transaction transaction :
                   getCurrentBlockChain().getLast()
                  .getTransactionLedger()) {
391                    if (!receivedBC.getLast()
                           .getTransactionLedger()
                           .contains(transaction)) {
392                        receivedBC.getLast()
                           .getTransactionLedger()
                           .add(transaction);
393                    }
394                }
395                receivedBC.getLast()
                   .getTransactionLedger().sort(
                   transactionComparator);
396                //we are returning the mining points since
                   our local block lost.
```

```
397                 setMiningPoints(BlockchainData
                        .getInstance().getMiningPoints() +
398                      getCurrentBlockChain().getLast()
                        .getMiningPoints());
399                 replaceBlockchainInDatabase(receivedBC);
400                 setCurrentBlockChain(new LinkedList<>());
401                 loadBlockChain();
402                 System.out.println("Received
                    blockchain won!");
403             } else {
404                 // remove the reward transaction from their
                        losing block and transfer
405                 // the transactions to our winning block
406                 receivedBC.getLast().getTransactionLedger()
                .remove(0);
407                 for (Transaction transaction :
                         receivedBC.getLast()
                        .getTransactionLedger()) {
408                     if (!getCurrentBlockChain().getLast()
                            .getTransactionLedger()
                            .contains(transaction)) {
409                         getCurrentBlockChain().getLast()
                            .getTransactionLedger()
                            .add(transaction);
410                         addTransaction(transaction, false);
411                     }
412                 }
413                 getCurrentBlockChain().getLast()
                        .getTransactionLedger()
                        .sort(transactionComparator);
```

```
414                 return getCurrentBlockChain();
415             }
416         }
417         return null;
418     }
419
```

As the comments in the code point out, this method starts by checking if both blockchains contain the same previous hashes. This means that they share the same blocks up until the last block. If this check fails, the null on line 417 is returned. Lines 383–386 check if the winning conditions for the received blockchain are met. If that is the case, then lines 389–402 get executed. What these lines do is as follows: we remove the reward transaction from our ledger, we combine the ledgers, we refund our own mining points, and then we add the winning blockchain with updated transactons in our database and set up the application state accordingly. The `else` on line 403 means that the winning conditions for the received blockchain were not met, which means our local blockchain won. Lines 406–414 remove the reward transaction from the received blockchain, add its transactions to our own ledger, and then return our blockchain.

The only method that remains to be explained from the `getConsensus` method is the `updateTransactionLedgers` method. Let's look at the following snippet:

```
310     private void updateTransactionLedgers(
            LinkedList<Block> receivedBC) throws
            GeneralSecurityException {
311         for (Transaction transaction : receivedBC
            .getLast().getTransactionLedger()) {
312             if (!getCurrentBlockChain().getLast()
                    .getTransactionLedger().contains(transaction) ) {
313                  getCurrentBlockChain().getLast()
                    .getTransactionLedger().add(transaction);
```

```
314                 System.out.println("current ledger id = " +
                    getCurrentBlockChain().getLast().getLedgerId()
                    + " transaction id = " + transaction
                    .getLedgerId());
315                  addTransaction(transaction, false);
316             }
317         }
318         getCurrentBlockChain().getLast()
           .getTransactionLedger()
           .sort(transactionComparator);
319         for (Transaction transaction :
                 getCurrentBlockChain()
                .getLast().getTransactionLedger()) {
320             if (!receivedBC.getLast().getTransactionLedger()
                   .contains(transaction) ) {
321                 receivedBC.getLast().getTransactionLedger()
                   .add(transaction);
322             }
323         }
324         receivedBC.getLast().getTransactionLedger()
           .sort(transactionComparator);
325     }
326
```

This method shares any transaction that might be missing between the local and the received blockchain from their last blocks between them. On line 311, we loop the transactions of the received blockchain's last block ledger. On line 312 we check if our local blockchain's last block ledger contains each transaction. If it doesn't, then we add it to our local blockchain and database. On line 319 we go through a second loop where we loop through our local blockchain's last block transactions. On line 320 we check if each transaction is contained in the received blockchain. If it isn't, then we add it to the received blockchain.

Lastly in this class we have some simple getters and setters, as shown in the following code snippet:

```
419
420     public LinkedList<Block> getCurrentBlockChain() {
421         return currentBlockChain;
422     }
423
424     public void setCurrentBlockChain(LinkedList<Block>
                        currentBlockChain) {
425         this.currentBlockChain = currentBlockChain;
426     }
427
428     public static int getTimeoutInterval() { return
                    TIMEOUT_INTERVAL; }
429
430     public static int getMiningInterval() { return
                    MINING_INTERVAL; }
431
432     public int getMiningPoints() {
433         return miningPoints;
434     }
435
436     public void setMiningPoints(int miningPoints) {
437         this.miningPoints = miningPoints;
438     }
439
```

```
440     public boolean isExit() {
441         return exit;
442     }
443
444     public void setExit(boolean exit) {
445         this.exit = exit;
446     }
447}
448
```

6.3 Summary

In this chapter, we covered the complete service layer of our application. We talked about singleton class design and how it fits our application. Next we covered methods that allow the functionality of our wallet and our blockchain. We learned how the functionality of our previous chapters is achieved by going over the implementation of the methods they use. One of the most important things we covered is the implementation of our blockchain consensus.

Here is a small recap of the topics in this chapter:

- Wallet functionality
- Using singleton classes
- Interface with JavaFX front end
- Blockchain functionality
- Implementations of the functionality of previous chapters
- Blockchain consensus implementation

Answer to question 6-1: The method `updateTransactionLedgers` on line 298 will be called.

Answer to question 6-2: Both blockchains are identical; the message on line 302 gets printed in console, and the received blockchain gets returned on line 307.

CHAPTER 7

Extras

This chapter will cover how to set up and run our blockchain application. We will also talk about topics and ideas for expanding the functionality of our application and conclude the book.

7.1 Running the Application

In previous chapters, we mentioned that we won't expose our application to the Internet because of security reasons, and instead we decided to test it locally. To do this, first let's create several copies of our `e-coin` project folder, as shown in Figure 7-1.

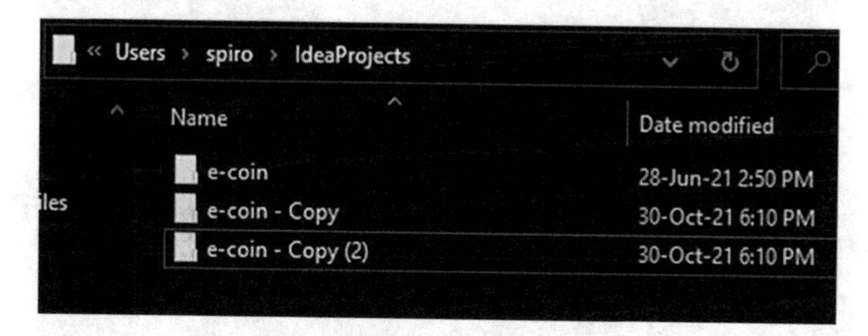

Figure 7-1. *Creating copies of the e-coin project*

The next step is to open each project in IntelliJ. You can do this by selecting File and then Open Project, selecting the other folders, and when prompted choosing to open a new window. You can look at Figure 7-2 and Figure 7-3 as references.

S. Buzharovski, *Introducing Blockchain with Java*,
https://doi.org/10.1007/978-1-4842-7927-4_7

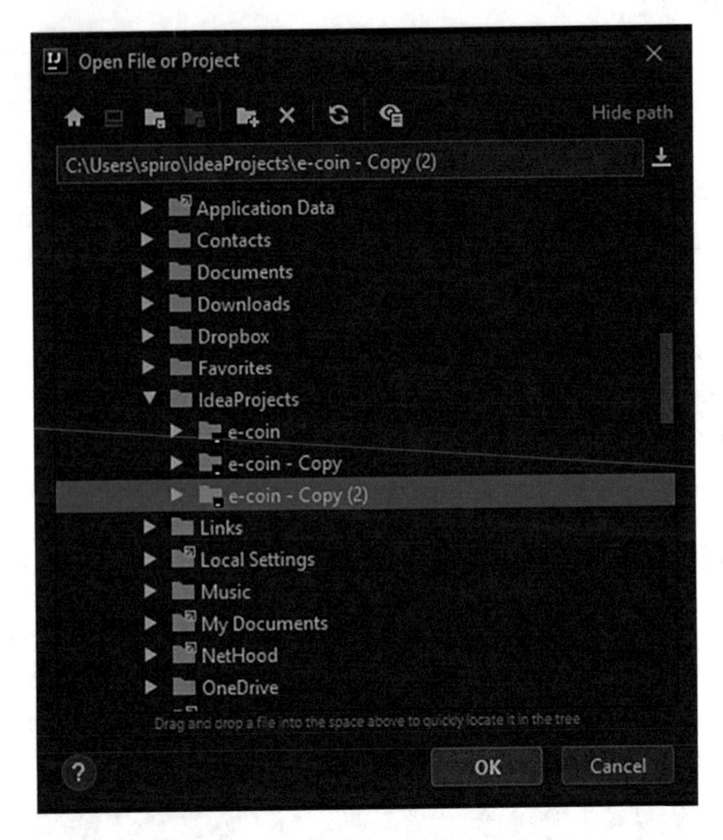

Figure 7-2. *Navigating to a folder*

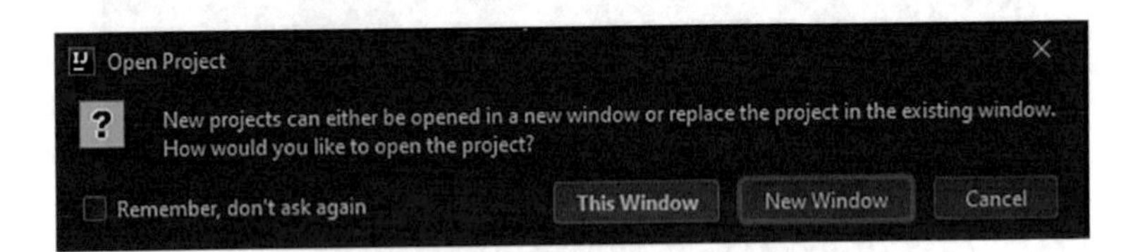

Figure 7-3. *Opening a project*

Once this is done and you have all your copies open in IntelliJ, it's time to change some of the hard-coded values to make sure each copy is its own original peer. First let's change the `PeerServer` port, because each peer needs to have its own port number. See Figure 7-4.

```
25      @Override
26      public void start(Stage primaryStage) throws Exception {
27          new UI().start(primaryStage);
28          new PeerClient().start();
29          new PeerServer( socketPort: 6000).start();
30          new MiningThread().start();
31      }
```

Figure 7-4. *Changing the PeerClient port*

Next we'll need to add the socket port numbers of the other peers to each other's `PeerClient` queue inside the `PeerClient` class constructor, as shown in Figure 7-5.

```
19      public PeerClient() {
20          this.queue.add(6001);
21          this.queue.add(6002);
22      }
```

Figure 7-5. *Adding the socket number*

Lastly, we'll need to go over the `jdbc` connections and change the file path to correspond to the file path of our copies. Figure 7-6 shows an example of one.

```
33      @Override
34      public void init() {
35          try {
36              //This creates your wallet if there is none and gives you a KeyPair.
37              //We will create it in separate db for better security and ease of portability.
38              Connection walletConnection = DriverManager
39                      .getConnection( url: "jdbc:sqlite:C:\\Users\\spiro\\IdeaProjects\\e-coin\\db\\wallet.db");
```

Figure 7-6. *Changing the file path*

The rest of these connection file paths can be found in the `init()` method of our `ECoin` class and in several methods in the service layer classes `BlockchainData` and `WalletData`. This last change will make sure that each peer will have its own databases for storing the blockchain and its wallet. If you want to export your wallet to another peer, you can simply copy the `wallet.db` database from one peer's folder path to another. Also keep in mind that if you delete a `wallet.db` database and you don't have a backup copy, that wallet's access and coins will forever be lost to you since you will be losing your key pair. Beyond this you just need to run each copy from within IntelliJ and you will have yourself a running peer-to-peer network.

Before running the application, make sure that you have Java SE 8 installed before running the application. If you are not sure what version you have, you can check it by typing `java -version` in the console of your IntelliJ.

Once you have mined some coins, you can actually send them to another peer by copying the other peer's address from their UI and using it in the Add New Transaction window, as represented in Figure 7-7. Observe that until consensus is reached for the current block, the coins won't appear in the receiving account. This prevents double spending because the consensus algorithm will check for attempts at double spending before assigning the coins to the other peer's account.

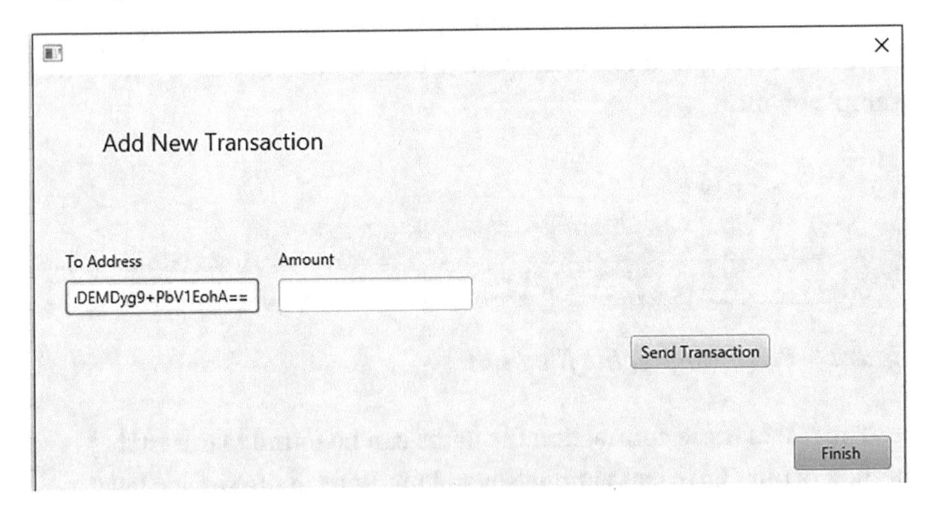

***Figure 7-7.** Adding a transaction*

Other functionality would be to stop one of the peers, let its blockchain get old (older than one to two minutes), and then restart it and observe how everything syncs up. Lastly, you can stop everything and check the databases with SQLite Developer. This should provide you with additional insight and confirmation of how the data is stored, and you'll have a great overview of the whole blockchain you have just created. Things should look similar to Figure 7-8 and Figure 7-9.

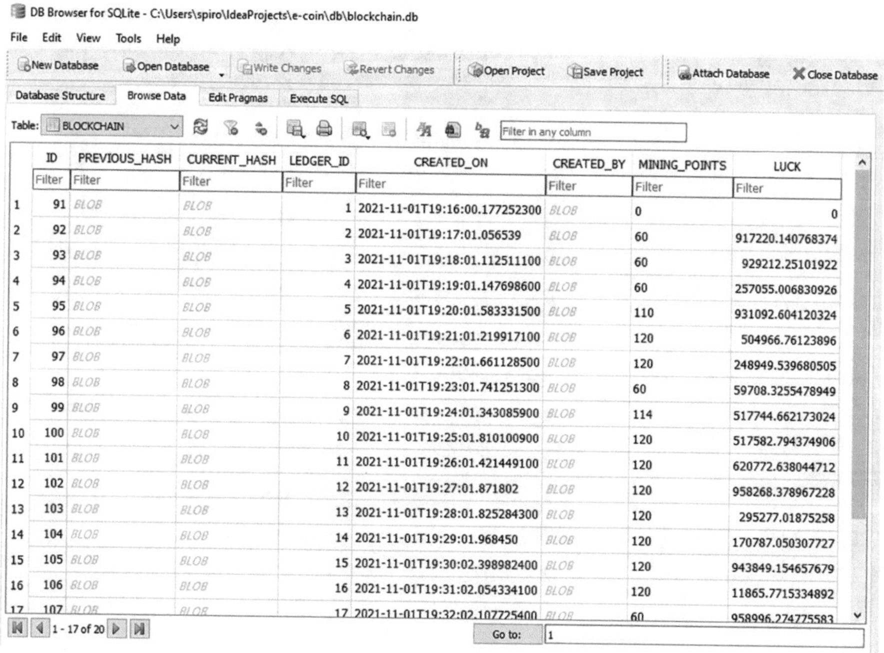

DB Browser for SQLite - C:\Users\spiro\IdeaProjects\e-coin\db\blockchain.db

File Edit View Tools Help

New Database | Open Database | Write Changes | Revert Changes | Open Project | Save Project | Attach Database | Close Database

Database Structure | Browse Data | Edit Pragmas | Execute SQL

Table: BLOCKCHAIN | Filter in any column

	ID	PREVIOUS_HASH	CURRENT_HASH	LEDGER_ID	CREATED_ON	CREATED_BY	MINING_POINTS	LUCK
	Filter	Filter	Filter	Filter	Filter	Filter	Filter	Filter
1	91	BLOB	BLOB	1	2021-11-01T19:16:00.177252300	BLOB	0	0
2	92	BLOB	BLOB	2	2021-11-01T19:17:01.056539	BLOB	60	917220.140768374
3	93	BLOB	BLOB	3	2021-11-01T19:18:01.112511100	BLOB	60	929212.25101922
4	94	BLOB	BLOB	4	2021-11-01T19:19:01.147698600	BLOB	60	257055.006830926
5	95	BLOB	BLOB	5	2021-11-01T19:20:01.583331500	BLOB	110	931092.604120324
6	96	BLOB	BLOB	6	2021-11-01T19:21:01.219917100	BLOB	120	504966.76123896
7	97	BLOB	BLOB	7	2021-11-01T19:22:01.661128500	BLOB	120	248949.539680505
8	98	BLOB	BLOB	8	2021-11-01T19:23:01.741251300	BLOB	60	59708.3255478949
9	99	BLOB	BLOB	9	2021-11-01T19:24:01.343085900	BLOB	114	517744.662173024
10	100	BLOB	BLOB	10	2021-11-01T19:25:01.810100900	BLOB	120	517582.794374906
11	101	BLOB	BLOB	11	2021-11-01T19:26:01.421449100	BLOB	120	620772.638044712
12	102	BLOB	BLOB	12	2021-11-01T19:27:01.871802	BLOB	120	958268.378967228
13	103	BLOB	BLOB	13	2021-11-01T19:28:01.825284300	BLOB	120	295277.01875258
14	104	BLOB	BLOB	14	2021-11-01T19:29:01.968450	BLOB	120	170787.050307727
15	105	BLOB	BLOB	15	2021-11-01T19:30:02.398982400	BLOB	120	943849.154657679
16	106	BLOB	BLOB	16	2021-11-01T19:31:02.054334100	BLOB	120	11865.7715334892
17	107	BLOB	BLOB	17	2021-11-01T19:32:02.107725400	BLOB	60	958996.274775583

1 - 17 of 20 | Go to: 1

Figure 7-8. *Browsing the data*

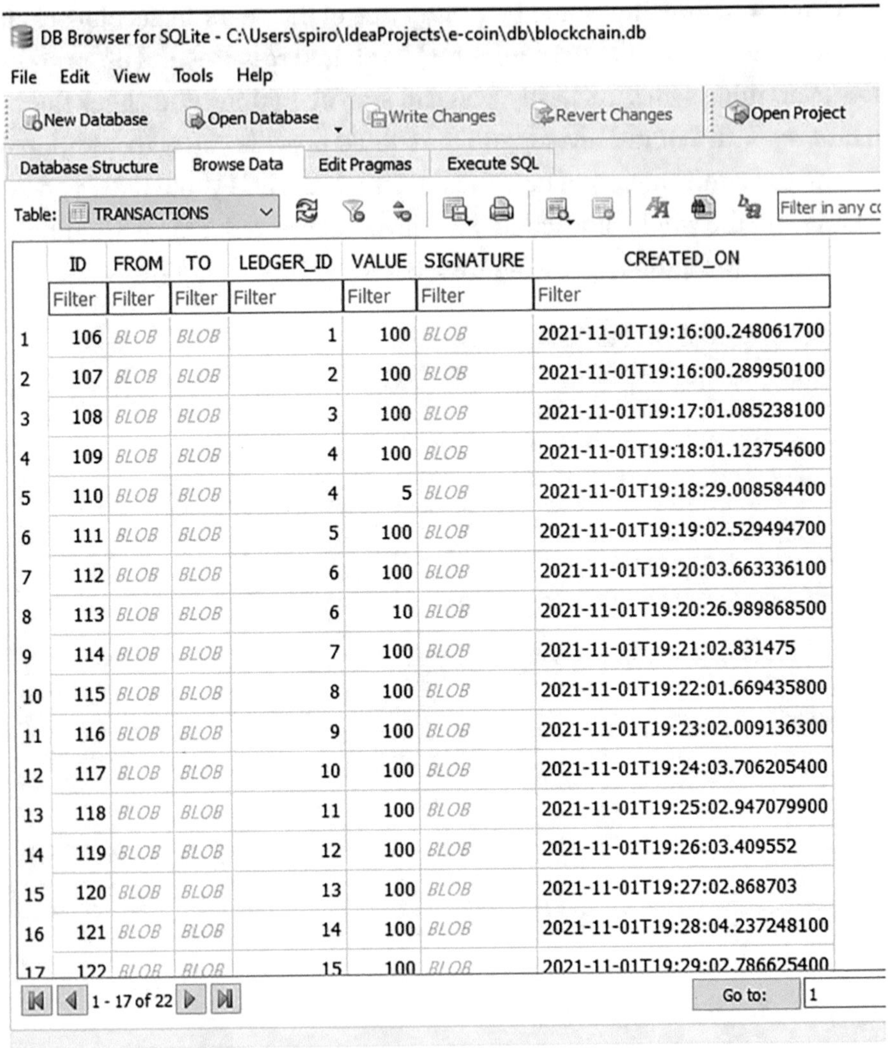

DB Browser for SQLite - C:\Users\spiro\IdeaProjects\e-coin\db\blockchain.db

File Edit View Tools Help

New Database | Open Database | Write Changes | Revert Changes | Open Project

Database Structure | Browse Data | Edit Pragmas | Execute SQL

Table: TRANSACTIONS | Filter in any c

	ID	FROM	TO	LEDGER_ID	VALUE	SIGNATURE	CREATED_ON
	Filter	Filter	Filter	Filter	Filter	Filter	Filter
1	106	BLOB	BLOB	1	100	BLOB	2021-11-01T19:16:00.248061700
2	107	BLOB	BLOB	2	100	BLOB	2021-11-01T19:16:00.289950100
3	108	BLOB	BLOB	3	100	BLOB	2021-11-01T19:17:01.085238100
4	109	BLOB	BLOB	4	100	BLOB	2021-11-01T19:18:01.123754600
5	110	BLOB	BLOB	4	5	BLOB	2021-11-01T19:18:29.008584400
6	111	BLOB	BLOB	5	100	BLOB	2021-11-01T19:19:02.529494700
7	112	BLOB	BLOB	6	100	BLOB	2021-11-01T19:20:03.663336100
8	113	BLOB	BLOB	6	10	BLOB	2021-11-01T19:20:26.989868500
9	114	BLOB	BLOB	7	100	BLOB	2021-11-01T19:21:02.831475
10	115	BLOB	BLOB	8	100	BLOB	2021-11-01T19:22:01.669435800
11	116	BLOB	BLOB	9	100	BLOB	2021-11-01T19:23:02.009136300
12	117	BLOB	BLOB	10	100	BLOB	2021-11-01T19:24:03.706205400
13	118	BLOB	BLOB	11	100	BLOB	2021-11-01T19:25:02.947079900
14	119	BLOB	BLOB	12	100	BLOB	2021-11-01T19:26:03.409552
15	120	BLOB	BLOB	13	100	BLOB	2021-11-01T19:27:02.868703
16	121	BLOB	BLOB	14	100	BLOB	2021-11-01T19:28:04.237248100
17	122	BLOB	BLOB	15	100	BLOB	2021-11-01T19:29:02.786625400

1 - 17 of 22 | Go to: 1

Figure 7-9. *Transactions table*

7.2 Topics for Future Improvements

Here are some ideas for you to consider if you decide to keep working on the application:

- For consensus, implement bitcoin's proof-of-work algorithm.
- Implement a proof-of-stake algorithm.
- Implement smart contracts.
- Implement support for nonfungible tokens (NFTs).
- Add wallet functionality to the UI such as import/export and creation of wallets with seed phrases.
- Make the full blockchain traversable through the UI; currently that's only possible through browsing the database.
- Add a toggle to turn on/off mining while maintaining the ability to send coins.

7.3 Conclusion

First I want to thank you for reaching the end of my book. What was covered in this book by no means exhausts everything that can be said regarding blockchain technology, but it is my sincere hope that it has provided you with solid fundamentals and a better theoretical and practical understanding of blockchains while using basic Java. The application as you can see is by no means a finished product, but it is functional enough to be a nice learning tool that you can use to experiment on and further your learning on your own. If by now you have started getting ideas of how to improve and rewrite pieces of the code by using your favorite frameworks and libraries, I'll consider that this book has served its purpose.

Index

A

B

S. Buzharovski, *Introducing Blockchain with Java*,
https://doi.org/10.1007/978-1-4842-7927-4

C

D

E, F, G

H

I

J, K

L

M

N, O

P, Q

R

S

T

U, V

W, X, Y, Z

Printed in the United States
by Baker & Taylor Publisher Services